The Anatomy of Freedom

Judge Harold R. Medina

The Anatomy of Freedom

by Judge Harold R. Medina

Edited by C. Waller Barrett

New York
Henry Holt and Co.

Published, September, 1959
Second Printing, October, 1959
Third Printing, March, 1960

Library of Congress Catalog Card Number: 59–11352

The author wishes to thank the following for permission to reprint in this
volume previously published speeches:

Chapter 3 from *The Meaning of Freedom* by Harold R. Medina, published by Freedom Fund, Inc., New York, copyright, 1958.

Chapter 10 from *The Spiritual Quality of Justice* by Harold R. Medina,
copyright, 1957, by the School of Law, Washington and Lee University.

Chapters 4, 12, and 15 from *Judge Medina Speaks* by Harold R. Medina,
copyright, 1954, Section of Judicial Administration, American Bar
Association; published by Matthew Bender & Company, Inc. By permission of the American Bar Association.

85652–0119

Printed in the United States of America

To my father,
Joaquin Adolfo Medina,
born in the city of Merida, Yucatan, Mexico,
on November 27, 1858.
In loving and grateful
remembrance

Preface

WITH a certain amount of independence and an uninhibited disposition I think I started life as a natural born nonconformist. In consequence I received the kicking around that was my due, and this did me a lot of good. In the course of time I became a lawyer and a law teacher and then a judge. As I look back over forty-five and odd years of this experience I protest against the view of some that the law is dull. My life has been exciting, almost adventurous at times, full of ups and downs, defeats and victories, and altogether rewarding and lots of fun.

Foolishly, perhaps, at the time of my so-called retirement on March 1, 1958, I told a reporter that I hoped to publish some of the speeches I had made in the last few years before various educational, patriotic, and bar association groups. Shortly thereafter an editor of Henry Holt and Company was busily engaged in persuading me to transform these addresses into essays. I resisted for a time, but soon found that most of the original text could be preserved, and, where much the same subject matter had been treated in various ways on separate occasions, there was opportunity for consolidation and revision. The easy, extemporaneous style of some of the pieces has been retained.

As the work of revision proceeded I suddenly noticed that these addresses, which contain more than a little biographical data used for purposes of illustration, traced a development that had been taking place within me over the years, all unnoticed. There was a common theme running through them all, a sort of melody sometimes definitely perceptible, sometimes subdued and all but silent—never absent. Hence the title: *The Anatomy of Freedom*.

Beginnings always have a special and peculiar significance; and it seems to me that as concerns the particular subject matter of this volume my whole cast of mind and the dynamics of my life go back to three men above all others. The first was Christian Gauss, a teacher of Romance languages and later the Dean of the College at Princeton; the second was Woodrow Wilson, who was President of Princeton during my four years as an undergraduate; and the third was Harlan Fiske Stone, who taught me at Columbia Law School and was the Dean during my early years of teaching there. My relationship with Gauss and Stone was one of real intimacy. But as I worked with and listened as a student to each of the three I supposed what they were giving me was certain valuable information and techniques in the subjects they were teaching. It never occurred to me that each in his own characteristic way was giving me lessons in the anatomy of freedom. Gauss started working on me when I was a freshman, young enough for impressions to cut deep. He was a true liberal; his mind was always open to new ideas, but they had a way of fading out under the scrutiny of his mild but ruthless analysis and criticism. It was he who taught me how to think. His father left Germany in the eighteen fifties or earlier to seek freedom, and when he found a house available in Ann Arbor, Michigan, on a street named Liberty Street, that settled it; the Gausses came to rest there. Many fortuitous circumstances brought our families together over the years. He thought I had made a mistake going into the law, and I thought so too when the decision was made, as the green pastures and lovely vistas which opened up before me in a career of teaching Romance languages and seeing Christian Gauss every day were beguiling and almost irresistible. It was only at Commencement in 1951, just after Harold Dodds had handed me my precious parchment as a Princeton LL.D., that Gauss put his arm over my shoulder and whispered, "Harold, I guess you did the right thing." It took him a long time to come around to that point of view.

Woodrow Wilson planted other seeds. They lay dormant and

slowly germinated and grew all unbeknown to me. Part of the anatomy of freedom, as I understood it, is spiritual and it is described in the teachings of Christ again and again, if only we open our minds to His message and His doctrine. The impact of the trial of the Communist leaders in 1949 brought this home to me; and my thinking on the subject was made more mature by participation in the Freedom Programs of the Protestant Episcopal Church at the Cathedral of St. John the Divine in New York and Christ Church Cathedral in New Orleans in 1957 and 1958.

The influence of Chief Justice Stone was of a quite different character. While all three men were fighters for freedom, Stone was solid and immovable; there was nothing volatile about him. He was no enthusiast, but he had a way of penetrating a maze of irrelevant procedural entanglements and finding and sticking to fundamentals. And he never failed to recognize the right of all concerned to speak their minds. His work with the conscientious objectors during World War I particularly left its mark upon me. With all his open-mindedness, he brought to every problem he was called upon to solve a shrewdness and practicality that made him impervious to shallow novelties and nostrums dressed up in the apparatus of freedom. He knew the real thing when the moment for action and decision arrived, as it often did in his experience both as Dean of Columbia Law School and as Associate Justice and as Chief Justice on the Supreme Court.

Practically everybody thinks he knows what freedom is, and there is an abundance of talk of our "liberties" in terms of glittering generalities. Tyranny and oppression have been under attack from the earliest times, but they still seem to thrive like the green bay tree. As usual, exhortation and the giving of unsolicited advice have accomplished little save to generate heat and breed controversy. It is my experience in life that the approach on the bias, the teaching by indirection, is the most effective. That is the purpose of this little book. The various essays often seem to relate to everything under the sun but the subject in hand. Remember, however, dear reader, that we are not giving an exposition of our American "freedoms" and "liberties," but trying to get underneath the surface in order to examine *The Anatomy of Freedom*.

I am grateful to Henry Holt and Company for persistence in

inducing me to recast the material into its present form and for their encouragement and advice; and I owe a special debt of gratitude to my friend, Clifton Waller Barrett, President of the Grolier Club, who is really the father of the project.

HAROLD R. MEDINA

United States Courthouse,
New York City.
August, 1959.

Table of Contents

The Anatomy of Freedom

1 A Look at America

I'm going to give a little background for some of the things I want to say about America by way of the things that happened during the Communist trial that are not generally known. When I started in there and was given the assignment, I said yes without any particular misgivings. Judge John C. Knox called me in and told me he had assigned the trial to me, and I said yes, and I walked out. I never have said no to an assignment yet. But I didn't have any particular notion that it was going to be more than a sort of rough-and-tumble. I really didn't know what a Communist was. That's the plain truth of it. I thought of them as sort of roughnecks who wanted to divide up our property and have a good time with it, but that was about all.

A few days before the trial, however, I got a little clipping that was sent to me from a Washington paper by Raymond Moley. You remember he used to be one of the Roosevelt brain trusters, and he was an old friend of mine. We worked on the faculty together at Columbia. He taught political science and I was on the law faculty, and I knew him very well. And this little clipping was to the general effect that

Harold Medina was a pretty good lawyer and a colorful figure at the Bar, but pretty soon he was going to wish he had never been born. Well, he didn't make any comment at all, but I knew that Ray Moley wouldn't send that to me unless he wanted to tip me off that there was something coming that I better get ready for.

Well, what could I do? There was no way of getting ready except that I paid pretty careful attention to the Sedition Trial. I don't know whether you remember that. It lasted for seven or eight months in Washington, and Judge Eicher, who was the judge, one day went out in his chambers in the middle of the afternoon and laid himself down and died. There had been an awful lot of hell-raising in that trial, and he had done a lot of things, and I started reading up on the Sedition Trial. I got everything I could get that would indicate what had happened. There were several books about it, and a good deal in the way of transcripts of records and so on, and that is all I did to get ready.

We started in, and I won't go into a long palaver about the threats to shoot me and all that sort of business. That happened pretty regularly. They never bothered me at all. I figured that if somebody was going to shoot you, he wouldn't write a letter to you and tell you you were going to get shot tomorrow morning at ten o'clock, and that's what they generally said. There would be some girl, supposedly in a bar or grill, and she heard the fellows in the next booth saying, "Joe, have you got that revolver of yours all fixed up, because we've got to pick the judge off tomorrow morning?"

The other fellow would say, "What judge?"

"Why, of course, Judge Medina."

So that went on for a long time, but I didn't pay any attention to it. And the deputy police commissioner came around and said they were going to give me some protection.

I said, "Well, take your protection and go along with it. There is no use dramatizing this thing and advertising around about it, and making it look like something big, and all this and that. Just forget about it."

Well, the next day he was back again and he said, "Now, Judge, you know your business, don't you?"

I said, "Well, I know a little about it."

He said, "Well, we know our business, and you're going to get the protection and we don't want any back talk."

Well, I understood that kind of talk all right, and so from that time on the FBI men, the city detectives, the state troopers—well, you know, at first, it was kind of exciting. We rushed out to our country place Friday afternoons with a state trooper ahead and an FBI car behind, and the sirens going. But I noticed when they got the people out of the way, they didn't know there was anybody behind the state trooper, and, boy, these drivers would cut right back in and I pretty nearly got picked off two or three times. So I had to keep about ten or fifteen feet behind this trooper's car, going about sixty-five or seventy miles an hour. And every old nail, pebble, or whatnot in the road got thrown up on my windshield, and by the time the trial was over I had to get a new windshield—you couldn't see through the darned thing.

But seriously, it is a pain in the neck having somebody watching you all the time. It sounds exciting, it sounds like fun, but every time you go to brush your teeth somebody is watching to see if you make out all right, and they are always pulling down the shades and running around. I guess it didn't do my wife much good. I noticed whenever the photographers were around the grandchildren would sort of disappear. And I found out that the mothers of these little kids were afraid that if their pictures appeared in the paper that maybe these Commies would kidnap them, and they were constantly on the qui vive about that. And from my standpoint I didn't want those little kids to grow up being afraid, having their mother tell them, "Now, if somebody comes to see Grampy, you just sneak off and come back home and get

3

in your room," or something like that. I tell you, if I had to go through life being afraid, I would rather be dead.

Well, we got in the trial and I was batting these motions out and having a pretty good time for a few days. Then the first thing that put me wise to what was coming was one day I got down somewhere around quarter past eight and there was a delegation waiting to see me. A delegation of workers from some place in Ohio. And there was another delegation right behind the first one. "Well," I said to myself, "these fellows can't do this sort of thing. I will explain this to them myself."

So I got the delegation in and I said, "Now, you boys can't do this. What are you coming in here for?"

"Well, this is a political case and you ought to throw it out. The indictment is all wrong."

I said, "Now, look here, you just can't do this. This is America. What would you think if I let some rich man or some political leader come in and tell me what to do with a case? You fellows get out of here. I don't want you ever doing this again." Well, my goodness, you could hardly get them out. Each one blah, blah, blahed, each one putting in his two cents worth, and as soon as I got them out there was another delegation. I tell you, these delegations of workers, delegations of veterans, delegations of purple-hearted veterans, delegations of housewives—they came from New England, from Oklahoma, from Mississippi, from out in the Far West, from the Middle West, from the Dakotas, from everywhere—and they were on my neck there for three or four days. Two days I went without my lunch. I would go down in the courtroom, finish up the session there, come up, and there were delegations waiting. I kept that up until all of a sudden I said to myself, "Why, Harold, you poor fool, you are just wearing yourself out here. There is no use doing this because they are all saying the same thing." I was going through the same routine, having a hard time getting them out of my chambers. I should

4

never have seen them at all. But I thought I was there representing America, and I didn't want Americans to be doing this sort of thing. And so I said, no more delegations. It was just as though you turned off a faucet. I don't know whether they came from all these places they said they came from. I believe they did. Then for the first time I realized the blue chips were down; that here was a force much greater than anything I had suspected; and that they were trying to knock me out and break up that trial.

As the stakes were high, I girded my loins to go ahead and go through, and of course the stakes were these: Was the American traditional method of doing justice equal to the trial of Communists? That was the issue. A big issue, because, if they succeeded in knocking me out, or in having some mistrial come about, then they could do it the next time, and the next time, and the next time. And you never, according to our Constitutional and traditional methods of administering justice, could convict a Communist. That was what I saw then was the issue, and then I went on this routine of mine. And, you know, they have the babies brought up that way; to put them to sleep at a certain time, feed them a certain time, and all this. Well, if you want to conserve your physical and intellectual energy, put yourself on a schedule so that exactly at a certain time each day you do what you have to do to go through that day, including that nap that I started taking after I ate my lunch every afternoon.

Every six weeks about, they would start a new line on me. When this business about the delegations didn't work, then they started the discrimination line. Now, in my whole background, my bringing up, my life taken as a whole, from the time I went to public school in Brooklyn, there were lots of Negroes, lots of Jews, lots of people of different races and religions. I mixed in with them. It never made a particle of difference to me. I really have no ill will or prejudice or discriminatory thoughts against anybody because of their race, or their religion, or their nationality, or anything of that kind —and I could prove it to you in many, many ways.

But, anyway, they started calling me the great discriminator in the courtroom there. I hated the Jews, I hated the Negroes, I hated this, I hated that—well, by that time I had got so that I just sort of smiled at them from the bench. I wasn't going to get sucked into a lot of debate and argument about that. Every once in a while I would say, "Now, remember, there is going to be a day of reckoning for some of you fellows. You better be careful." But I didn't get annoyed or angry. But outside of the courtroom they got up these handbills with a picture of me looking like a sort of demon, and then had it down that I hated the Negroes, I hated the Jews, I was the great discriminator. So-and-so said I was the great discriminator. They put these handbills in people's pockets in the subway when they weren't looking. They slipped them in automobiles that were parked, particularly if they were old, dilapidated-looking automobiles. They took them around to the apartment houses in the poorer sections of the city, and they slipped them under the doors at night.

Then I began getting repercussions. People began writing in to me: "Why, Judge, you seem like such a nice man. Why do you hate the Negroes? Why do you hate the Jews?" Well, you know, you would say how can a normal person be bothered by a thing like that? Well, hang it all, if you are continually accused day in and day out of being just the particular kind of person that you don't like, that you don't want to be, that you know you're not; you don't like it. And, furthermore, here is where the subtlety of it comes in. If you are an honest man and you look into your own consciousness and you say, "I wonder. Could it be that they are right? Could it be that I am fooling myself, that I really think I have none of this prejudice but maybe I have?" You see, you take a man who has no integrity, who is not honest with himself, and all

6

those things roll off like water off a duck. But you take an honest man who isn't sure—we judges are not sure that we are right when we decide things, we do the best we can—we worry about those things. And so I worried and fussed about that. But nothing happened and that just helped to wear me down a little, I suppose.

Then we got along, and the first real big effort they made to break up the trial was one day when one of the defendants was on the stand and he was being cross-examined. The United States attorney put a question to him and his lawyer objected, and he pleaded his Constitutional privilege to refuse to answer.

I said, "Well now, Mr. Witness, you didn't have to take the witness stand but you did. You testified on direct examination and questions on cross-examination that are relevant to those you have to answer because you waived any rights about refusing to answer those. But I'm going to think about this overnight. I don't want to make a mistake. And you talk to your lawyer overnight. This is something I want to do with care and thoughtfulness."

So, the next day we were back there again. It was Friday, the third of June, 1949. I shall never forget it. When I went in there that morning you could just feel something in the atmosphere. You know when you feel the hair on the back of your neck going up a little bit, you know there is something going on. You don't know just what it is. And all day in the courtroom the place was full of these Commie sympathizers. They would get in the line about eight o'clock in the morning, and the minute they opened the doors of the courtroom these fellows would all rush in. There might be half a dozen people who were friends of some of the judges and got in the front row, but almost everybody in the courtroom, except the reporters, were sympathizers, and I felt that something was going to happen there. I didn't know what it was. Anyway, we got back on the job, and to my surprise the United States

7

attorney withdrew that question that had been asked the day before. But pretty soon he was back with another one that was even clearer. And so they objected, I overruled the objection, the witness refused to answer, and I said, "Now, you haven't got any Constitutional right to refuse to answer this question at all. I hereby direct you to answer that question."

He said, "I refuse."

I said, "I hereby sentence you to imprisonment for thirty days for contempt of court in my immediate view and presence, unless you sooner purge yourself by answering the question."

Well, what happened then you just wouldn't believe could happen in an American courtroom. That whole courtroom rose as one man; the yelling and shouting and hullabalooing that went on, you never heard such a thing. The marshal and the deputy marshals started running around, coming from different parts of the courthouse. I sat there just as quiet as I am now. Somebody was helping me that day, let me tell you without any doubt. And I looked around and I said, "Isn't this Mr. Hall?" Well, it sure was Mr. Hall, and he was shooting off his face plenty. I said, "Mr. Reporter, Mr. Hall said thus-and-so, thus-and-so. Mr. Hall, I remand you for the balance of the trial." And then I said, "Isn't this Mr. Winston? Mr. Reporter, Mr. Winston just said so-and-so, and so-and-so, and so-and-so. I remand you, Mr. Winston, for the balance of the trial." All this time this shouting and yelling and hullabalooing was going on, and I picked off about four of them. Then the noise quieted down. Mind you, I hadn't raised my voice; none of this gavel banging, no shouting, nothing of that kind; all very quiet. And there they were still standing, and Dennis was right in the middle. He started in at me. I said, "Mr. Dennis, don't you remember? I said I was going to treat you as one of the lawyers. You are your own lawyer here. If you think something you say now is going to get you in jail with your friends, you're making a big mistake because you can say

whatever you want and I'm not going to put you in jail today."
I said, "Mr. Dennis, if you want my opinion, you really look
silly." Well, he did look silly, and he didn't like the idea of
that. He wanted to go on, but he didn't know quite what to
say. I had been suggesting that these people sit down, two or
three times. They hadn't paid any attention to me. So I said,
"Mr. Dennis, why don't you sit down?" Well, he didn't want
to sit down. "Well," I said, "you know, you can stand up if
you want to." Well, with that he said, "Sit down." They all
went down just like a bunch of German storm troopers taking an order. That was the end of that crisis for the moment.
They had expected the trial to break up that day. If I had
carried on as I suppose under my ordinary steam I probably
would have, well, it would have broken up. One thing would
have led to another, and you never could have got the case
going again. So, that Friday I went off; and remember all I
had said was, "I remand you for the balance of the trial," to
each of these fellows whom I had sentenced to imprisonment.
So the next Monday morning we came back and everything
was serene during the morning session. We went on with the
trial, and then after lunch, as I came back to go on the bench,
all the lawyers were ready for me in that little room that was
behind the courtroom. They had a very important communication.

I said, "What is it?"

Well, one of these lawyers representing the Communists
said, "We argued this morning the writs of habeas corpus to
free those men whom you tyrannically and illegally imprisoned last Friday. Those were argued before Judge Leibell
this morning, and the Judge has formulated certain questions
for you to answer."

I said, "What are they?"

"Oh," said the lawyer, "they are in this envelope."

I said, "Let's open it."

He said, "No, Judge Leibell said that you are to take that

on the bench and open it and answer the questions in open court."

Well, you can imagine what I thought of Judge Leibell at that particular moment. As it turned out, it was a very wise thing for him to do. It was the only thing for him to do. But at that moment I said to myself, "Here I am alone, isolated, with fifteen or eighteen other federal judges right here in my own courthouse, and they give me a sealed envelope to answer and tell me to get on the bench, where everybody can look at me when I open it, and answer the questions." It seemed a little bit too much. Of course, I could have opened it, nobody could have stopped me, but I just wasn't going to give those men the satisfaction of showing the white feather. So I said, "All right," and I put on my robe and I went out, ascended the bench, opened the envelope, and there was question number one:

"Did you remand the defendants so-and-so, and so-and-so, and so-and-so, as and for a criminal contempt?"

Two: "Did you remand those defendants in the exercise of your plenary powers as a trial judge to revoke bail?"

Three: "Did you imprison them for any other reason, or in the exercise of any other power?"

Well, I hadn't thought, to tell the truth, and now I had to do some quick thinking. I looked down at these men and oh, that look that I saw so often when they thought they had me in a pickle was right there. "Well," I said, "I imprisoned those defendants for a criminal contempt of court, and in the exercise of my plenary powers as a trial judge to revoke bail, and in the exercise of each and every other power I possess under the Constitution and laws of the United States." The smiles were gone. I could have answered it wrong. It happens there is no decision in our circuit giving the trial judge the absolute right which he possesses in our state courts to revoke bail and send a defendant on trial back to prison during the

10

trial without giving any reason. In our state courts they have that power. But in our circuit of the federal courts it has never been decided. Perhaps bail may be revoked only if it appears likely that the defendant will jump bail. If I had answered differently then we would have had some more appeals. And I had plenty of appeals going on. Of course, they appealed from these writs: the denial or dismissal of the writs of habeas corpus. They appealed the time they wanted to have a certificate that I was prejudiced against them, but they didn't win a single one of the appeals from the beginning to the end; the main judgment, and all the other judgments, and all the miscellaneous ones. Well, anyway, we were over that.

So then we got along into the summer, and I was getting tireder and tireder of these birds picking on me there all day long; all day long dropping these torpedoes, as I call them— these propositions of law. They had a whole crowd working these things up all night every night, and then they would pop them at me all day. I was keeping my eye on the jury, and keeping these fellows away from the jury box. I really was having a time.

Well, we got along. I guess the first thing they tried on me—remember how Forrestal jumped out of that window in the hospital? Well, about a month after that the pickets down in that little park in front of the courthouse began carrying some new signs, and they read: "Medina will fall like Forrestal." Well, that sounds funny. But they followed it up: telephone messages, "Jump. Jump. You've got to jump," letters, postal cards. Well, do you know, it was the only thing that really worked on me. It seems ever since I was a child I had been afraid of height. I had had this awful feeling of wanting to jump. I remember when I went to Niagara Falls with my father when I was sixteen years old, and I didn't dare go anywhere near the edge where everybody else was looking over and watching the Falls because I had that awful feeling of wanting to jump.

11

I tell you, it was years before I got over what they did to me during that period of about a month or six weeks on that particular "jumping out the window." I remember when I got up to our apartment and was going to bed at night, Mrs. Medina would put those big windows up. Whammo! they would go up there in our bedroom, and I would say, "Eth, please, please put those down." She thought I was fooling. She couldn't believe that I really meant it. And yet as I lay there in bed I had this feeling of wanting to get up and run for that window and jump out. I tell you the men who thought this up were demons. They were positively demons. And if you remember how many times in Russian history people have jumped out windows—you remember Masaryk in Czechoslovakia? Remember that Russian schoolteacher who jumped out the window in the Russian Embassy in New York? There was a lot of talk that she jumped out to escape. Maybe, maybe not. She didn't die, but lots of others in Russian history have. And, just think, if you are all alone in their custody and they are working on you! I used to think they pushed the people out the window. But they don't need to do that. When they get working on you the way they know how to do, you jump out by yourself—you don't need to be pushed.

Then, nothing came as a result of that, and they started with signs: "How do you spell Medina? R A T." Well, nothing came of that. So then a few days after that, that whole crowd, out in that little park in front of the courthouse, maybe two or three hundred people, began to chant, "Judge Medina is an S.O.B. Judge Medina is an S.O.B." Just think, in our great United States of America, two hundred people out in front of the courthouse singing and chanting that sort of thing. They weren't doing that to get me angry. They knew they couldn't get me angry that way. They had been calling me that about ten different ways all day every day in the trial without actually using the words. So that wasn't it. They were slick. The reason they tried the "How do you spell Medina?

12

R A T" was the same thing, but that didn't get the reaction; but this "Judge Medina is an S.O.B." business, that brought it.

I got letters, telegrams, telephone messages from all over the country, many of them from judges in our state courts in New York, from friends of mine, saying: "Harold, what is the matter with you? Haven't you got any guts? Are you going to sit there and let these fellows do this sort of thing right in front of the courthouse and disgrace our administration of American justice? Are you going to sit there without any backbone, and not put those fellows in jail for contempt of court for doing that?" Why, that was just what they were begging for. They had me hanging on the ropes then. I was tired. I was tired. I had enough trouble handling what I had to handle in the courtroom. All I needed to do to knock myself out was just about half a dozen or ten or fifteen contempt proceedings against those pickets. Why didn't the other judges do it? Why me? I had my hands full.

Another thing was the isolation of my position. I was alone. I had to be alone. Judge Leibell had to do what he did, because that demonstrated that we judges weren't doing any conniving about this or working up any phony rulings. I was the man there in charge, and I had to be alone. The other judges in the courthouse couldn't start contempt proceedings without perhaps muddying the waters, mixing things up one way or another. As it turned out, how much better it is that they proved to the American people what they were by doing these things day after day. I would have accomplished nothing by contempt proceedings except to knock myself out, and that was what they were trying to do.

A little while after that—and this is the last one I am going to tell by way of background, oh, I guess it was about the twentieth of August, about half past three in the afternoon. I just felt faint. I felt dizzy. I couldn't go on. I was afraid I would faint and fall off the bench. And so I said, "Gentlemen, I don't feel well. I'm going to take a little recess."

The men down there right in front of me looked up as much as to say, "Well, we've got him now; this is the end. This is what we've been waiting for, boys."

When I went out to that little room behind that courtroom, I honestly didn't think I was ever going back. I felt terrible. I lay down on that little couch and I did some tall praying that afternoon.

Some people have faith, and some people haven't any faith. I was just one of the lucky ones. Ever since I was a child I had really believed, and I prayed. The only night I didn't say my prayers was the first day I was at boarding school. I remember it very well. I had this new roommate in my room, and all the excitement, and I didn't say my prayers. But that was the only time. I had this resource. I had my faith. And I really meant business that afternoon all right.

I had been doing a lot of praying during that trial. Not just when I went to bed at night, but little prayers during the day. Just keeping in touch with God and asking Him for strength and guidance. Well, I didn't have any visitation or feel any thrill go through me as though the Spirit was within me, but pretty soon I felt refreshed and strong enough to go back. And I did go back, and I went on to the end of that trial.

Now we come to the look at America. After the trial was over, I went down to my chambers to clean things up and say good-by to the staff, and then those letters began coming in. You would hardly believe it—bales! You can get an awful lot of letters in a bale. There were thousands and thousands and thousands and thousands of them. They were all over the chambers. Some postal cards, some telegrams, but mostly letters. And I just started to get to work on them. I got two stenographers back from my old law firm, and I had my secretary there in the courthouse, and I had these three girls working in shifts. There I was reading these letters and throwing them away, and answering maybe two or three out of a hundred. Maybe there was a letter from some elderly person, or some blind person. Many of them came from blind people who had somebody write for them and I would answer those. Some were voices from my boyhood. I had forgotten who these boys and girls were that I went to public school with. A letter would come from one, and from another, and from some of the teachers I had had at prep school, whom I never would have dreamt even noticed I was in the school. I did this for two or three days, and all of a sudden—I don't know how many thousands of them I had thrown away before I woke up—I said, "Why, Harold, you're in the midst of a spiritual experience here. Here is the whole United States of America spontaneously reacting to a spiritual influence, a spiritual force that makes them do this." And that is what it was.

All over the country these people had to write me. It wasn't fan mail. They weren't telling me what a wonderful fellow I was. I was just a symbol. I meant to them for the moment the country they loved, the administration of American justice that they revered so, and it had been vindicated, it had triumphed, and they wanted me to know that they cared. Those letters were so intimate. Over 2,000 of them came signed by the man and his wife together. I don't think I ever heard of that being done before. And yet, here were these people, thousands of them, who wanted to be on that letter together. They wanted me to know that they, that particular husband and wife who loved each other so much, loved America too. And they said in effect, "Judge Medina, notice us. We care. We care. We love America, too, and we want you to know." There was that intimacy about them. They would come from all kinds of little businesses: filling stations, restaurants, little shops of one kind or another; and each one would be down with his name and what he did there. I remember one from a Greek restaurant and there was the boss, not at the top; it was the dishwasher that was at the top and the porter and the assistant porter and the assistant dishwasher and the boss's name was mixed up somewhere in the middle. They didn't let him get either at the top or at the bottom. He was just one of the hoi polloi, and no fooling.

A telegram came from a hospital that all the patients in the hospital signed. And then it got down to the nurses' desk and all the nurses signed. Not just the nurses of such and such a hospital, but Mary Jones and Mary Smith. And then it gets over to Western Union and the Western Union girls put their names on, too. They wanted to be in on it. They wanted me to know.

In that movie called *Lili* where there is a puppet show in a circus, this little girl who is so lonesome and feels as though nobody cares at all is singing to the puppets. And then you see the background, the people in the audience who were watching. One of them will say, "I care." And another one will say, "I care." And that is the way it was with me there. All these messages came and each one was "I"—"I care. I care about America, Judge, just like you do, and I want you to know." That happened not only with these letters but with people. If I should live to be a thousand years old I would always be grateful for the experience that I have been through. Now, mind you, that is six years ago. You would think people would have forgotten. But the American people, the ordinary common man, the fellow I call the little guy— and I'm one of them, just like the rest of them—they know. They know more than you give them credit for knowing.

And so, when I was out in San Francisco, I was walking along the street there. This was, I guess, fairly close to the end of the trial or maybe six months or a year after it, and there was a worker sitting in one of these funny little cable cars with his lunch box and dust all over his clothes. He had evidently been working on some sort of building operation. He took one look at me and he hopped off the car and came over and he gave my arm a squeeze and looked right in my face. He never said a word, but I have never heard a speech so eloquent as he made to me. I knew what he was saying, and he knew too. And then he ran back and hopped on the car again. The same car he had hopped off. He wasn't looking for anything from me. None of these people could get anything from me and they knew I wasn't looking for anything from anybody else.

Ever since that trial I have been careful not to let the taint of money come in on anything I have done. It would have been so easy to run around making lectures at $1,000 a night. One fellow offered me a contract, $50,000 a year to go around making lectures and telling about the Communists. Well, there are a lot of people in this world that won't do things for money, a lot of them. I'm not the only one. And I haven't sullied my reputation or that of America by ever consciously doing anything that would take advantage of what came with these letters and with these people talking to me.

Only last week I was going down Forty-third Street and along came a taxicab with four or five passengers. The driver jammed on the brakes, jumped out of the cab, came over and said, "Judge, would you mind shaking hands with me? I've a lot of respect for you."

I said, "Why, I'm glad to." I don't know what the people in the cab thought, and I don't give a hoot. It was nice.

The day after I was made a circuit judge, put on the Court of Appeals, I was going out of the apartment house, getting into my car, and two carpenters ran up from a building operation up the street, and one of them put his arm around my shoulder and said, "Judge, we're glad you got a raise." And he was glad.

And wherever I go, I have people come up to me to shake my hand or to pat me on the back, not looking for anything. They don't want anything from me. They know I'm not looking for anything from anybody. The relationship is pure. There is nothing selfish about it either way around.

Well now, what is the moral of all this? I draw this moral.

17

I think if you go back to the time that our country was founded, the people came here from all over the world, for what? For spiritual values. That's what they came for. They wanted freedom. They wanted justice. They wanted a chance to show good will. Have you ever thought that those three things are great, dynamic spiritual forces? Now, just think of it. Good will. Practically every religion has as part of its tenets, "Love thy neighbor as thyself." How different our lives would be if we really did that. I think the friendship of one man to another is just about the most precious thing there is in this world. I love my friends. I've got a lot of friends. You don't make many new ones after you are young, and, you know, with friendship the big thing is not what you get for yourself but what you do for your friend. How you help him when he is in trouble. You don't care whether he is in the wrong or not, or whether he has perhaps committed some breach of the law, or whether when he has trouble with his wife maybe he is wrong about it—you love him, you want to help him. That's friendship, isn't it? You never think about what you get for yourself, and so that is the way with this good will business. It is a spiritual force. It is traditional with us. Nothing annoys me as much as all this talk that Americans are money grubbers, and all they care about is money. Of course we work hard. We are industrious. We want our families to have the good things. We want our children to have a good education. But this idea of our not having any interest in spiritual things is wrong. That is just what America stands for. Good will and freedom and justice. Those are the things that these people were so excited about when they wrote me these letters and when they came up and patted me on the back and spoke to me and so on. Whatever else happens to me in life, they can't take that away from me.

2 The Influence of Woodrow Wilson on the Princeton Undergraduate, 1902–1910

1956

I had thought at first that I would write my "Personal Recollections of Woodrow Wilson at Princeton"; but I have changed it to "The Influence of Woodrow Wilson on the Princeton Undergraduate, 1902–1910," which gives me more elbow room and affords opportunity for an appraisal of certain qualities of Woodrow Wilson that have been all too seldom stressed.

I have done everything within reason to make my data authentic. Indeed, the process of preparation has been a significant experience. After working, with the assistance of Mr. Dix, the Librarian, and Mr. Clark, the Curator of Manuscripts, and their staffs, in the Firestone Library for a few days on the original letters and miscellaneous writings of this great man, I felt like a pygmy as I started for home. Old memories hidden away in the back of my mind were stirred, and I now see, as I never saw before, how he has influenced my life and stiffened my backbone at critical times.

What I purpose doing is: first to state the undoubted fact of what he meant to the men of my time in Princeton, and then to try to explain how this came about.

So let us roll back the curtain of history, forget the governorship, the presidency, the first great war, and the League of Nations and take ourselves back to Princeton in the fall of 1905 or thereabouts.

Everyone on the campus called him "Woodrow"—not to his face, of course—and he was our hero. It was infinitely more than popularity. He seemed surrounded by an aura of destiny. We hung on his words as on those of our inspired and incomparable leader. We still think he is the greatest university president there ever was anywhere; and we are everlastingly grateful that we spent four full years under the spell of his eloquence. There are many here today who can testify to the accuracy of this seemingly extravagant statement. What was the source of his power over us?

Again and again before he became president of the university in 1902 he was voted the most popular member of the faculty. This was doubtless due in large measure to the extraordinary vitality of his lectures and the deftness and the humor with which he dealt with late-comers and with dogs and with a whole miscellany of unexpected occurrences in the classroom. With his brown derby, riding here and there on his bicycle, he was a familiar figure. On one occasion, I am told, he pedaled across the campus in all the regalia of a top hat, frock coat, and striped trousers. Once I was greatly impressed with a statement by him that he bought a new tuxedo every year.

While often distant and severe, and always dignified, he had an inexhaustible fund of wit and humor; and he was a great storyteller, specializing in stories about Negroes and socialists, with a liberal sprinkling of personal reminiscences and limericks. They gave a dance at Prospect one evening and we boys sat around in his study so long listening to his storytelling that Mrs. Wilson came in and chased us out, as the girls had been waiting for about three-quarters of an hour.

That he was kindly and considerate and helpful is attested by a host of anecdotes; and many members of my class were on terms of intimacy with him. Some of them loved him dearly; and I heard one of them say the other day that "Woodrow" was a second father to him. His personal letters are indisputable evidence of a warm and affectionate nature.

But, giving due weight to all this, I think we must look elsewhere for the explanation of our devotion to him. He was no hail-fellow-well-met, nor was he a Mr. Chips, nor did he make friends easily with the undergraduates or others.

Here is what he writes of himself to his classmate Frank C. Garmany on April 2, 1879, while still in college: "I, perhaps, am colder and more reserved than most of those who are fortunate enough to have been born in our beloved South; but my affection is nonetheless real because less demonstrative."

Were we grateful for the preceptorial system and for his valiant and successful efforts to raise the standard of scholarship at Princeton? Perhaps, in a few individual instances. We vaguely sensed that the good old days were supposed to be over; but I doubt very much if more than a fraction of the class ever did more than half a day's real work, except just before examinations. We heard all he said about not letting the side shows run the circus; but it got out that he had once said, "The Constitution of the United States guarantees to a man a certain amount of loafing; otherwise it would come under the head of cruel and unusual punishment," and we thought that was fun. No one ever dreamed that undergraduates might, should, or could work the way they say they do now. We were chasing one another around so fast trying to get on the extracurricular activity bandwagon that it was years later before most of us realized how right he was.

But how he could talk! And we flocked to hear him at Whig or Clio, at Murray-Dodge, in the pulpit quite often on Sundays, and on all sorts of miscellaneous occasions. What a spellbinder he was! At first we were fascinated by his perfect diction and the skill with which he chose just the right combination of words to express his meaning. Pretty soon it dawned on us that what he had to say was important. There was no mistaking his sincerity: he spoke with a singular intensity, he was always quoting from the Bible, and bit by bit he got his spiritual message over to us. I never saw a man who could say the same thing in so many different ways.

Let me give you the general idea first and then follow up with a few examples. He kept telling us to be good soldiers of Christ and to endure hardships, that the hardest thing in the world was to be a real Christian, that principles and ideals were the only things worth fighting for. He explained that the mere pursuit of individual interests was the road to obscurity and frustration, that in a country of free citizens the welfare of the commonwealth springs out of the character and the informed purposes and the action of the private citizen. He kept talking about America all the time, the duties of citizenship, democracy's desperate need for leaders, for men who really believed in equality of opportunity and an understanding of other people, irrespective of worldly wealth and social position. And finally we got the impact of his thesis that spiritual strength meant power.

Moral principles, ideals, action, achievement, power; all these spelled out to us in the words of Christ, with continual emphasis upon unselfishness and sacrifice, the peace and good will to men which went beyond one's own borders and reached out to all mankind, and the unending fight against what he called "the thraldom of evil."

Can you imagine what all this meant to us boys! Here was a man who really believed in unselfish devotion to one's country, who was seeking, in the words he quoted from the Bible, to "prove what is that good, and acceptable, and perfect, will of God," and to lead us out of the wilderness into green meadows where ideals and principles were formulated and acted upon. This is what young people craved to hear in 1909, it is what they crave to hear now, and it is what they will always crave to hear.

And Woodrow Wilson never let us down. He was consistent from beginning to end. He never compromised on a matter of principle, indeed he told us that "on a principle a man has no right to yield."

Let me give you a significant example of his consistency. One of his favorite parts of the Bible was the First Psalm. Here are the six verses in full:

1. Blessed is the man that walketh not in the counsel of the ungodly, nor standeth in the way of sinners, nor sitteth in the seat of the scornful.

2. But his delight is in the law of the Lord; and in His law doth he meditate day and night.

3. And he shall be like a tree planted by the rivers of water, that bringeth forth his fruit in his season; his leaf also shall not wither; and whatsoever he doeth shall prosper.

4. The ungodly are not so: but are like the chaff which the wind driveth away.

5. Therefore the ungodly shall not stand in the judgment, nor sinners in the congregation of the righteous.

6. For the Lord knoweth the way of the righteous: but the way of the ungodly shall perish.

He liked to talk about the tree planted by the rivers of water which bears its fruit in due season. One evening he told us it was interesting to think that every man has his season; and then he went on to say, "Nothing is guaranteed of the tree, only the fruit. It is neither here nor there what becomes of a man's person." This was in 1908 or 1909. I got it from a compendium of the diary notes of one of my classmates who passed away many years ago, which was loaned to me confidentially.

Compare this with the following report of a dialogue between the President of the United States and his physician a few days before the collapse which brought to an end his fight for the League of Nations, as reported in Gerald W. Johnson's *Woodrow Wilson: The Unforgettable Figure Who Has Returned to Haunt Us.*

Grayson was worried out of his wits, but the President stubbornly adhered to his schedule. What if it did kill him? He had seen battle fields where brave men had died by thousands in this cause. Was he to quit because to fight on was dangerous? The question silenced the doctor but did not lessen his anxiety.

Woodrow Wilson, as I have said, was a stickler for just the right word in the right place. Two of his most famous speeches have been confused in the minds of Princetonians. The first was "Princeton in the Nation's Service," delivered in 1896 at the Sesquicentennial Ceremonies, and the other, "Princeton for the Nation's Service," in 1902 when he was inaugurated as president of Princeton. The one looked back and other looked ahead. This was another instance of the consistency and unity of his character. He was always telling us, "You are either going forward or you are sliding backward. There is no such thing as standing still." And he spoke of the generations behind us crying us on to do better things than otherwise we could even attempt, and "generations beyond" calling us on "to a day of happier things."

Of those who heard it, who will ever forget his 1908 Baccalaureate Address on "The Free Life"? Are there any Princeton men of my time among my readers? Do you remember the Princetonian banquet in the spring of 1909, when Woodrow Wilson made Arthur Brisbane look sick, with his talk about making money in the newspaper business? Do you remember the last time we as undergraduates heard him speak, when he told us about the unprofitable servant, quoting from St. Luke, "We are unprofitable servants: we have done that which was our duty to do"? That was the synthesis of all his teaching, the "secret of what it is to live," by launching out into the paths beyond the call of duty. And that night when he was the sole speaker at our senior banquet when he spoke for over an hour on social justice? It made our blood tingle for a long, long time.

Yes, this is the explanation of our reverence for Woodrow Wilson. He is a continual and effective disproof of the widely held fallacy that men do what they do for material reasons. And it is well to keep in mind the fact that the things of the spirit, including freedom and justice and tolerance, brought our beloved republic into being, and spiritual qualities will rule our destiny in the future.

Those who remember their Horace will know the opening lines of what is perhaps his most famous poem:

> *Exegi monumentum aere perennius*
> *regalique situ pyramidum altius*

I have built me a monument more lasting than bronze, higher than the royal pile of the pyramids.

And a few lines later,

> *Non omnis moriar, multaque pars mei*
> *vitabit Libitinam*

I shall not wholly die. A great part of me shall escape the goddess of the funeral pyre.

And so the spirit of Woodrow Wilson lives on; he lives in my words here, and in a thousand voices of devoted citizens grown old in the service of their country; beckoning us to the heights beyond the call of duty, encouraging us to be steadfast and immovable in support of the principles and ideals he taught us, and bidding us to fight on forgetful of ourselves, for Princeton and for America, under the banner of Christ.

3 The Meaning of Freedom

1958

There are certain basic aspirations common to every member of the human race; they well up from deep within us. One of these is freedom. Freedom is, I suppose, in a large general sense, the result of lack of restraint; and so there are those who, viewing the matter superficially, confuse freedom with unbridled license. It requires little argument, however, to demonstrate that no society of men could long survive if every person could do precisely what he wanted to do, including stealing, lying, and otherwise interfering with the orderly and proper business activities and recreation of others.

On the other hand, it seems clear to us Americans that there is something precious and unique about every single human being that is entitled to respect and protection. This is often referred to as the dignity of man. One individual may wish to devote his life to music or painting, another to agricultural pursuits or to philosophical speculation, or to any one of thousands of other physical or intellectual occupations. If each human being is different from every other, which is clearly the case as we see it, each individual must be permitted to decide for himself the kind of work he wishes to do, the religious doctrines he wishes to accept, the family ties and responsibilities he wishes to assume, and where he wishes to go to work and live. And, if each individual is to be permitted to make and carry out all these decisions, he must also be permitted later to change his mind, to leave one type of work for another, or to change his place of residence from one part of the United States for another, or to change his religion and so on. The particular individual may do some foolish things, he may make some unwise decisions; but, from our standpoint as Americans, life would not be worth living if we had to get permission from some government official before we could change our occupation or our residence or make and carry out other decisions affecting our personal life. And the notion that the government, by propaganda, by a carefully constructed series of rewards and punishments, and at times by outright compulsion, should control our education and our thinking and our beliefs is absolutely abhorrent to us.

In the aggregate, however, the activities of man are carried out in a setting of laws in the general welfare and for the well-being of the people as a whole. These laws affect a multitude of aspects of community and national life. Some of these laws define interests in real and personal property, the rights of landlords and tenants, and the power to make wills and to inherit property; others affect a great variety of matters of health and sanitation; civil and criminal penalties and liabilities are established with the general intent of promoting the happiness and contentment of all the people in every community. Naturally there are differences of opinion as to the wisdom or efficacy of one or another of these various laws. And that is precisely where another very important feature of American freedom comes into play. Our system of government is based upon federal and state legislative bodies with the power to pass the various laws just described, and the very essence of our system is the election by popular vote of the members of the legislature who are to pass these laws. In some parts of the United States one political party is in the ascendancy and in other parts another, but the scene constantly shifts and political contests for these seats in the legislature are constant and they are bitterly fought. Sometimes the electors do not make the wisest choice of a legislative representative, but the correction of such mistakes is within the power of the same voters when the time comes around for the next election. The control of the entire executive and legislative branches of the government is at all times in the people and this control is real and demonstrable. When we Americans hear that under some other political system the ballot to be cast by the voters has only a single candidate for office, selected by some group with authority to make the selection, we view such an election as a fraud on the people. The fact that the candidates for public office run without opposition demonstrates, in our view, the complete lack of one of the basic essentials of freedom.

There are times, however, particularly times of crisis, when the great majority of the people are convinced that certain new laws should be passed. It is in time of distress and tension that large numbers of people become panicky and they are apt to demand the passage of laws infringing on the basic principles of freedom. It is right at this point that the American Constitution steps in and calls a halt. One of our greatest freedoms is the protection of minority groups against the demands of the majority of the moment. There are several of these constitutional safeguards, but the principal ones are set forth in what we call our Bill of Rights, the first eight amendments to the Constitution, passed virtually at the time of its adoption. Thus no law may be passed affecting the right of the people to worship according to their conscience, or depriving any person of his life, liberty, or property without due process of law. Freedom of speech and of the press is preserved inviolate. There are various provisions of the utmost consequence protecting individuals against the oppression of government officials: no one may be compelled to give evidence against himself in a criminal case, excessive bail is strictly prohibited, prosecution must be based on a specific charge formulated according to existing law, all *ex post facto laws* are forbidden, and the right to trial by a jury of one's peers as well as the right to counsel for one's defense are made inviolate.

These and other mandates of the Bill of Rights are often referred to by Americans as an integral part of their "liberties" or their "freedoms." And it is perfectly clear that, sheltered by these Constitutional guarantees, no person could be whisked away in the small hours of the night and taken off to prison without even knowing the nature of the charge against him, without any right to obtain his liberty by posting bail, and without the right to a lawyer of his own choosing to advise him and to defend him. The possibility of the arrest of a person and his confinement for long periods of time, hidden from his friends and relatives and wholly at the mercy of government officials, simply does not exist in America. Moreover, the provisions of the Constitution as a whole make it impossible for any group to seize power and promptly change the whole fabric of government. No matter how overwhelming may be the victory of a political party at a particular national election the basic constitutional scheme remains intact.

How is this system made to function? How is one to be sure that these Constitutional provisions are not mere empty words, speaking in terms of freedom but wholly without substance or actuality? That is where the courts and the judges come in. When a judge is invested with office he takes a solemn oath to uphold the laws and to maintain the Constitution. And one of the ways by which the judges do this is to regard the government, in civil or criminal cases coming before the judges for decision, simply as one of the parties in the case. It would be an offense of the gravest nature for the executive or any agent or representative of the government prosecutor privately to attempt to dictate to or even advise a judge of the reasons of policy or political expediency or anything else that made it necessary or desirable that the judge should decide any case according to the wishes of the executive. What often seem to be technical decisions, difficult for laymen to understand, are merely the warp and woof of the fabric of Constitutional law which develops slowly to meet the particular problems of each age, but with an eye focused always and above all on the preservation of our "liberties" and our "freedoms" which constitute our most precious heritage.

4 The Celebration of the Eightieth Birthday of Robert Frost

1954

A few days after the conclusion of the Communist trial my old friend and Princeton classmate Bayard Dodge, who had for many years been President of the University of Beirut, came in to call. He said he had a word of advice: "Don't give in to these people who want you to make speeches, Harold, you will wear yourself out and the game isn't worth the candle." But, less than a week later he was back asking me to make a little speech of welcome to the delegates from the Near East countries to the United Nations. It seemed absolutely silly; and so I used as a rhetorical device for my brief address to the delegates the theme, Why on earth should Harold Medina be selected to welcome the dignitaries from Jordan and Yemen and so on. And that is what I shall do this evening.

It does seem incongruous that a mere minion of the law should help to celebrate the eightieth birthday of America's most distinguished man of letters. I have no license to discuss poetry and I shall not do so except by indirection. But I do have some qualifications which may be pertinent, although I rather suspect that none of them had anything to do with

31

my selection. In the first place, I am an honest-to-goodness humanist, trained in the disciplines of humanism, and that was "The Road Not Taken." I am an American and I have gone through an experience since the Communist trial for which I shall always be grateful; it has given me an almost unique opportunity to feel the pulse and the heart throbs of the great mass of those who are often called the "little people" of this country. And, finally, in a very small way, I am an artist; but as so often happens with lawyers and actors, the little pieces of my artistry have mostly gone with the wind.

Robert Frost is a creative artist of the first rank; his humanism has a touch of the universal in it; and he is above all an American.

It would be folly for me to attempt a recital of his Pulitzer awards, his medals and citations, his honorary degrees, and the innumerable ways in which his genuis has been recognized. Nor shall I quote his poetry or go beyond the field where I can speak my own mind without pretense.

Now, it seems to me that over the ages the only true historians are the creative artists: the sculptors, the architects and the painters, those who composed the folk songs and the liturgies and chants, and especially the poets. After all, the history we were taught in school about battles and the dynasties of kings and emperors, and all that, does no more than touch the surface. Deep down underneath, as man struggled from the mud on up toward the stars and civilization slowly made one advance after another, it has been the creative artists who truly represented the temper and the complexion of their times. It is they who have interpreted the yearnings and the intuitive desires of their countrymen; and there has remained intact, despite the ravages of time and all the forces of destruction, a true recording, however imperfect, of man's struggle.

Taking history as thus defined, I think there will be few here tonight disposed to dispute the fact that of all these creative artists who have accomplished so much, the poet stands out pre-eminent and on a pinnacle by himself. He can only know what it is human to know; he perceives only the persons and the things about him in his particular age and in the midst of particular circumstances. And yet with his divine gift of sensitivity and understanding it is his unique privilege to distill the essence and to give expression to the innate thoughts and urgings from within of the people whom he sees and with whom he talks as he goes about the business of living.

So it is that Homer and Virgil and Horace and Dante and others have made their times live again for us. But they have done much more. In some way or other they have come to represent and largely to influence and bring about that love of country which we sometimes call patriotism.

I often wonder whether Horace really believed what he wrote when he composed that ode beginning *"Exegi monumentum aere perennius."* But the fact is that he had built a monument more lasting than brass. There was something about his odes and epodes which stirred the souls of the Romans in his day and made them proud of their heritage.

In perhaps a subtler and more effective way Virgil did the same. You remember the theme line of the *Aeneid: "Tantae molis erat Romanam condere gentem."* And he added here and there a touch of pathos which we do not so often find in Horace. Once read it is difficult to forget that untranslatable line: *"Sunt lacrimae rerum et mentem mortalia tangunt."*

Can one doubt that Robert Frost is the greatest living interpreter of the spirit of America and perhaps the greatest of all time? There is no blare of trumpets and waving of the flag, none of that boastfulness of our prowess and our capacity for producing automobiles and bombs. But he has within his mighty grasp the spiritual qualities upon which our destiny depends.

I would have you ponder for a moment and help me check over the qualities of which he speaks so often. There is strength, endurance, and tenacity, coupled with tenderness, sympathy, and humility. There is delight at the man who finds happiness in his toil and the sweat of his brow. There is infinite good will and courage and a spirit of independence and self-reliance. All these are savored with the salt of wisdom and humor. Not the epigrams and rhetorical devices of some other clime, but wisdom and humor of the homespun variety. And throughout, a pathos which, at least to me, is unrivaled.

Yes, he is the interpreter of the spirit of America. He speaks for all of us; and as we listen and repeat his verses, there is action and reaction. Thus his power seems to come almost from within ourselves.

Perhaps the most significant feature of all his work is its universality. There is something infinite and timeless about his poems. And yet I truly believe that in this too he represents the best of America and that the reading of his poems will help us, not to attain some selfish end or to increase our wealth and power but, with other members of the human race, to take one further step ahead.

Probably everyone here remembers how it is a habit of Horace to soar to the heights and then suddenly dash off and finish a poem with some light turn or twist. That always used to puzzle me until I came to realize that this was just his way of telling us to keep ourselves in balance, that famous old golden mean he speaks about so often. And so I shall conclude with a lighter note.

I read in Sunday's paper that at a little party in Washington supposed to celebrate the eightieth birthday of our guest of honor he threw those in attendance into confusion by announcing that it really was his seventy-ninth. Perhaps he may do the same thing here tonight. But if he does, I beg leave to remind him that, after all, while he is a competent witness to his age, according to Wigmore, the testimony of others is entitled to more probative force.

It has been a great privilege for me to speak to you here this evening. I have done nothing to deserve this honor, but I appreciate it just the same. Thank you.

34

5 The Liberal Arts and the Professions

Building The Foundation For A Career
In One Of The Professions

1956

Let us examine the function of professional men in society and the ways in which the educational process may best develop the skills and techniques, as well as the qualities of heart and mind necessary for the task in hand.

Whatever one may think of Plato and the Pythagoreans and the very early days, there seems no reason to doubt that the phrases "a liberal education" and "the liberal arts," from the Middle Ages down to the present time, have had a connotation of freedom. For only a man whose mind is free may follow the path of truth wherever it may lead. And the pursuit of truth is the inevitable consequence of that never-to-be-satisfied curiosity which is one of man's most characteristic traits. Another such trait is the pursuit of happiness which our Declaration of Independence enumerates as one of our inalienable rights. Thus free men pursue the endless quest for the development of their innate capacities and in the process find their greatest satisfactions in their daily work. One of the secrets of life is portrayed for us in the New Testament parable of the talents where we are told: "For unto every one that hath shall be given, and he shall have abundance: but from him that hath not shall be taken away even that

35

which he hath. And cast ye the unprofitable servant into outer darkness: there shall be weeping and gnashing of teeth."

These simple, indisputable fundamentals lie at the base of our search for a formula to guide those who wish to use their college years to best advantage with a career in one of the professions in view. How blind one is apt to be to the fact that most of us get a large proportion of our pleasures and satisfactions from the performance of our daily tasks! And this is peculiarly true of professional men and women who, in their constant striving for perfection in their art or calling, develop their own particular talents to the highest possible degree, whilst at the same time ministering to the needs of others than themselves.

You will observe that I speak broadly. We are wont to think of professional men and women as doctors and lawyers, scientists, architects, and so on, but I shall speak of the professions in the broadest sense, as indeed I must, as we have professional schools of business and journalism, music and the arts, and what not else. If I seem to wander in the direction of the law that is only because that is my natural bent after forty-five years of exposure. But everything contained here is, in my opinion, applicable in varying degrees to each and every one of the professions.

So let us pause for a moment to consider the essentials of a liberal education, the sort of thing a university or college is supposed to do for a young man or woman, and check them off against the requirements of the professions.

Some of the functions of a liberal education have such a close relationship to each and all of the professions that I need do no more than mention them in passing, although vocational trends not infrequently obscure this relationship. Perhaps at the head of the list stands the discipline of the mind; for who can pursue any calling with success unless his powers of observation are so trained that he may see even the tiniest detail of each particular problem and then by some rational effort bring the seeming chaos into order, eliminate the irrelevant, and synthesize the rest. Without such discipline, which is stressed in every liberal arts institution worthy of the name, all is futility and confusion. The study of mathematics surely serves this purpose. And, for generations, the ancient Greek and Latin classics, with what I believe to have been an unfortunate overemphasis upon grammar and syntax, provided much the same sort of discipline. That is probably why the students, by and large, have such a dislike for mathematics and Latin. It is more pleasant to wander about in fields where one can ad-lib at discretion and where the answers to questions are not so disconcertingly right or wrong.

Then, too, one must be articulate. The art of communication is almost a profession in itself. First to think and then to convey the product of one's thinking to others, this is the task of the spoken and written words; and the study of languages and literature teaches us to embellish and illustrate so as not only to communicate our thoughts with clarity but also to instruct and to persuade.

There is a technical part of every profession that can only be mastered by those whose minds are truly disciplined and by those having the power to express their thoughts in terms clearly understood by their colleagues, by their patients or clients, and by the world at large.

But I would speak of another and perhaps an even more important phase of what I consider to be the function of a liberal education, something which may forever elude us unless it enters our subconscious before we commence our years of formal professional studies.

It is curious to see how little seeds, planted in one's mind in the most haphazard way, grow and develop. A few years ago some one gave me a copy of a biography of Dr. Harvey Cushing, the celebrated brain surgeon. The impression I had when I finished the book was that Dr. Cushing's greatest contribution to society was probably his two-volume *Life* of his friend and even more famous worker in the field of medicine, Sir William Osler, rather than his remarkable techniques in brain surgery; and I could hardly wait to get a copy, which I read with delight. These two men, in the midst of the crowded routine of busy professional careers, had found time to follow the paths of literature and to pursue the Muses in a way reminiscent of some of the craftsmen of the Renaissance.

Sir William was in great demand as a speaker and, on seemingly innumerable occasions, he gave little extemporaneous talks which contained, in many instances, the very quintessence of his wisdom. One of these was an off-the-cuff performance at a gathering of undergraduates at Yale. He talked on the subject of a liberal education, and he said that one of the primary functions of a liberal education was to teach good manners. What could he have meant by this?

Before I answer this question, I shall give an illustration or two by way of background. And I hope you will remember that I started speaking about seeds. We all know how often there is reference in the New Testament to the planting of seeds and the bearing of good fruit. The beautiful First Psalm in the Old Testament tells us about the tree planted by the rivers of water which bears its fruit in good season. One thing leads to another in this "best of all possible worlds" and all is growth and decay.

I started out as a humanist, and one of the most poignant experiences of my life came on the day when I decided not to pursue graduate studies in the Romance Languages and go back to teach at Princeton, but rather to follow a career at the Bar. I well remember when I first read the *Essays* of Montaigne as an undergraduate. He flitted here and there like a bird, discussing everything under the sun, but especially disclosing the personality and charm of the man himself. Here was a man who revealed himself completely, much after the manner of Pepys in his Diary, although Montaigne wrote for all the world to read if it chose. All humanity seemed to speak to me as I read those famous essays.

Some of you may recall that he had a young friend, Étienne de La Boétie, who died in his late thirties, and I was thus led to read La Boétie's *La Servitude Volontaire ou Le Contr'Un,* one of the books written way back in the sixteenth century, which planted some of the seeds of the French Revolution. And in *La Servitude Volontaire,* La Boétie commented on the fact that Frenchmen were the willing slaves of symbols in a most extraordinary way. One of these symbols was the oriflamme or pennant of France, which the flower of French youth had followed into battle for generations, and the other was *la sainte ampoule,* the vial which contained the sacred ointment, said to have been brought down from heaven by a dove at the time of the coronation of King Clovis, and this sacred ointment was used down through the centuries at the coronation of each of the succeeding kings of France. It was an interesting and provocative book.

And so I wondered what had become of *la sainte ampoule,* and I discovered that one day during the French Revolution there was a great concourse of people in Paris in an amphitheater, not unlike one of our great football stadia, and out in the open space in the midst of this throng was what looked like the butt of a huge oak. Suddenly a hush of silence fell upon the multitide and a big, burly man, who looked like a blacksmith, stepped forth, placed a small gray object on the butt, leaned back and swung a massive hammer, and *la sainte ampoule* was smashed to smithereens. The people shouted and danced and hugged one another and shouted, "Now, at last, tyranny is no more."

My readers will probably think I am a bit queer, but for years I have been taking courses in Latin by correspondence with an old professor named Dr. W. R. Bryan who lives in Valatie, New York. Now we are working on Livy's *History of Rome.* He starts with the fabulous stories connected with the founding of Rome and goes on, covering a period of over

39

seven hundred years. What changes! Mighty empires flourished and fell; the pristine virtues of an impoverished economy gave way to avarice, luxury, and widespread public corruption. And as he wrote, in the time of Augustus, Rome knew no such thing as freedom. Civil wars and upheavals had followed one another in rapid succession until at last tyranny ruled supreme.

At this point I wish to cut back a bit and bring a certain idea into better focus. I said that all is growth and decay. Another way of expressing this is to say that in this same "best of all possible worlds" all is change, every kind of change, sometimes slow and imperceptible, sometimes violent and sudden, like the destruction of a fortress or a social revolution.

I also remember the thrill of reading for the first time Cicero's *Pro Archia Poeta,* and the *Aeneid* of Vergil and Benvenuto Cellini's *Autobiography* and *Le Grand Cyrus*, one of those interminable French romances of the sixteenth century. These books, chosen almost at random, tell us about all kinds of people over a period of hundreds of years. They open up a vista to our mind's eye. Each represents its generation in a way, each seems so different from the others; the outward habiliments bear little resemblance to one another, but the characters portrayed are human beings like ourselves making their way through life in search of happiness or peace of mind or a sense of the fulfillment of their destiny or whatever else one may call it. There is pathos everywhere, and yearning. The very development of new words or phrases or methods of expression has significance.

My final illustration has to do with the last case I tried as a trial lawyer before I went on the bench. As is usually the case the principal issue was one of veracity with respect to what was said at a certain conference. The man who gave the version which I hoped would prevail had testified by deposition in Washington, just before leaving for the Pacific, where he was killed in action in World War II. In many ways his version was unsatisfactory. He said all he could tell was his best recollection, that he might be wrong, but that he thought the substance of the conversation was thus and so. The other participant was a blustering, self-confident man who testified in the most positive way at the trial. It was my task to convince the jury that this man was not telling the truth.

In my summation I quoted from the definition of a "gentleman" in the *Century Dictionary*. The word has several meanings, as you know, but the one which fitted into my case read as follows: "A man of good breeding, courtesy, and kindness; hence a man distinguished for fine sense of honor, strict regard for his obligations and consideration for the rights and feelings of others." My purpose was to contrast the two personalities and thus make the testimony of my witness appear more probable than that of the witness called by my adversary.

How often it happens that the pushy, self-confident, positive people are worsted by those of quiet deameanor, who seldom, if ever, resort to exaggeration and bombast and whose every word and act are characterized by courtesy and consideration for the rights and feelings of others!

We go through four years of college, picking up a little here and there, occasionally inspired to the point of ecstasy by some teacher whose precepts and ideas seem peculiarly in harmony with our own. We learn, our minds expand, our talents develop, and we leave the hallowed walls of our college a quite different person from the one who entered as a freshman.

One of the things a liberal education can do for each of us is to give us perspective. We peer back into the past as far as our gaze can penetrate; we look ahead into the future as far as we can see; we have opportunity to make acquaintance with the aspirations, the dreams and hopes and fears and doubts of all humanity. We read about the captains and the kings and the priests and the martyrs, the creative artists, the poets, and those who composed the chants and liturgies to charm the hearts and soothe the consciences of all succeeding

41

generations. Unless we are singularly obtuse we can scarcely go through this process without feeling the impact of spiritual forces and without some realization of the limitless strength and power which come to those who permit these spiritual forces to dominate their lives and lead them on to action for the betterment of their community and the nation.

Another thing we learn is to expect changes, changes in our own lives, changes in the complexion of society, the passing of pleasant, comfortable ways, and the sudden impact of a new and different world. We learn not to fear these novelties.

Surely a warm, sympathetic understanding of other people and a tolerance for the views of others, even when they differ radically from our own, is a mark of good breeding and good manners. For once these qualities have been developed, the inevitable consequence of their development is a kindliness, a good will, a courtesy and consideration of and toward other people which is of the essence of the life of a free and enlightened people. How important it is for us truly to appreciate the dignity of man, other men, each and every member of the human race be he or she young or old, wise or foolish, or even tainted with corruption and sin. If we understand and sympathize with other people, in their happy days and in their times of suffering and despair, we can help them.

The other day I was reading an address by one of the Jesuit fathers, the Most Reverend Thomas A. Boland, on "St. Vincent de Paul and Christian Education." Speaking of that great educator he said:

> He lays down the fundamental rule that the personality of the individual pupil is to be respected. Here he speaks as the experienced director of souls, convinced that the whole purpose of the education process is to bring the men to God and that each individual soul created by God has a unique personality which must be respected.

This is absolutely of the essence of the principle I am trying to expound. I would have the planning and the energies of our liberal arts institutions devoted primarily to the task of bringing about the fullest possible development and expansion of the innate talents and capacities of each individual soul committed to their charge, bearing in mind that each is unique and different from all the others.

Now, what has all this to do with laying the foundation for a career in one of the professions?

In the first place, a wide cultural background, as free as possible from the practicalities of vocationalism, gives us some conception of the universal; it widens our horizon and sharpens our vision; it gives us not only a sense of perspective but some understanding of how deeply we can penetrate into the bowels of a subject with concentration and persistence.

Then, too, everyone recognizes the importance of creative powers and imagination. Like other powers these are developed slowly; they respond to a multitude of stimuli. You remember my reference to the planting of seeds and the bearing of good fruit, and the parable of the talents. This is the same old story of growth and decay. In discussion of this same subject once I heard Woodrow Wilson say, "If you don't use your muscles, pretty soon you won't have any muscles." The principle is the same with the development of intellectual powers and creative powers and character building. Creative powers, imagination, integrity, steadfastness— I could enumerate a dozen more. These are just as much innate capacities as any others, probably more so. And if we are to develop these capacities to the utmost, we must constantly put them to use. That is why periods of daydreaming and meditation in solitude are so important. Thought processes, conscious or subconscious, come first; actions later.

About thirty years ago, and long before I became a judge, a man made an appointment to see me. I thought he was coming in to get some legal advice or to retain me in a case.

43

But he wanted me to help him with his son. He was a man of ample means, the executive head of one of our large industrial corporations, and he was willing to pay any amount if only I would agree to help him. He seemed surprised when I explained that helping boys and girls and their parents was an extracurricular activity for me, and that I didn't take money for that sort of thing.

Well, it seemed the boy was at Groton School where he was editor of the school paper, and he had become interested in writing fairy stories and allegories. This was gall and wormwood to the father, who wanted me to persuade the boy to give up writing fairy stories and get to work on the sort of thing which would make him a great lawyer or businessman.

"What do you want to do," said I, "make a freak out of your boy?"

"Yes," he replied, "a freak just like you."

The upshot was that I agreed to see the boy, but I refused to make any commitment as to what I would say to him. I never shall forget the day he came in. I suppose he expected me to bully him and tell him to give up writing the fairy stories. But I didn't. It was quite a time before he felt at ease; and then we talked about his father. I think he understood his father better when he left. Anyway, he kept on writing fairy stories for a time; and later made a good record at the Harvard Law School. The last I heard of him he was doing a fine job as a lawyer.

I would have a student go through the four years of college following his own bent with as little regard as possible for the professional career he is planning to undertake as his life's work. Many of these prescribed and recommended prelaw and premedical courses are mere diversions from the main stream of liberal arts studies. I do not say they have no utility, for of course they do, and they save precious time later. What is more, many a student will study these same subjects if you leave him alone. That is all to the good. But otherwise they necessarily interfere to some extent with the full development of these innate powers of which I speak, which form a reservior which we may tap at leisure for the balance of our lives.

The kind of a person one is inevitably has a lot to do with the kind of a doctor or lawyer or architect a man becomes. As I sometimes put it: "Be a man first and a lawyer next." What are sometimes described as inner resources are not mere hobbies to keep us busy after we retire. We must live with ourselves. Will the companionship be agreeable? What are we to think about, when we are not in our offices? What books will we read? Or shall we merely look at pictures in the magazines and at television and listen to the radio or do crossword puzzles? Shall we simply drift with the current of contemporary affairs, or will our lives be guided by ideals and moral principles? Who can deny that a true course of training in the liberal arts will help us to solve these perennial personal problems and bring us a measure of happiness which will be reflected in the performance of our professional duties?

Who can deny that these inner resources, these creative forces, and imagination are just as important to an artist, a journalist, a physicist, an architect, or a businessman, as they are to a lawyer and a doctor?

But the greatest contribution a liberal education can make to the lives of professional men or women is in the development of their spiritual powers. By all odds this stands at the head of the lot. A warm and sympathetic understanding of other people is a pearl beyond price. It is so easy to think of oneself and let the rest of the world go hang. Other people's troubles seem remote and unimportant. We speak of them kindly, but we do nothing effective to help them. Everyone is ready to cheer for good will, tolerance, justice, and freedom in the abstract. But how many, by attentive consideration of the effect of the lack of these spiritual qualities in individuals, in groups and communities, in nations and in whole civilizations, to say nothing of the impact of sectarianism in religion, have had these lessons burned into their very souls, so that there is an irresistible urge to put these spiritual qualities to work in their daily lives?

Do I speak of something remote from the actuality of professional life? Much more than technical skill is part of the trappings and apparatus of the life of a doctor or surgeon. How often are we told that the gentle understanding and sympathetic ministrations of general practitioners have saved countless lives. There is often that indefinable something about some specialists which tends to evoke that will to live so indispensable to survival in serious cases. Thus it is with the law. Our function in society is to serve, to help the weak and the oppressed, to vindicate the rights of all, especially the widows and the orphans and the destitute, and to preserve those freedoms and fundamental rights which constitute our liberties, even if to do so we enter the lists to defend those charged with the most infamous crimes.

There are those who think of lawyers as a rich and influential class, living the life of Reilly on the fat fees which roll in from legal work on corporate mortgages, mergers, and other large matters involving huge sums of money. But the reality is that any lawyer worth his salt is devoting the greater part if not the whole of his time to the helping of people in dire distress of mind or body. He is not supposed to shun the cases which involve emotional disturbances and often have a disagreeable and nasty factual background. A lawyer who without compelling reason refused to accept an assignment by the court to defend an indigent person charged with crime, or to protect the rights of an infant or incompetent, would soon lose caste among his fellows.

And the same principles apply in varying degree to those in other professions. How absurd it is to say that the spiritual qualities of which I speak have little to do with musicians or bankers or chemists or any of the others!

One of the fallacies most widely held is that people do what they do for purely material ends. All history gives the lie to this. The true fact is that the dynamic forces in our lives are spiritual. And this is peculiarly true of the professions, however appearances may seem to the contrary.

Perhaps some of you may be thinking, "Judge Medina, you are wandering from the point. What has all this to do with good manners?"

Well, I have been talking about good manners all the while, and in precisely the same sense as was intended by Sir William. But in the process I have pursued the technique of the advocate. That is my profession. What a fascinating task it is to write on your minds as it were, to go up and down, over and across, weaving the warp and woof of the tapestry of an idea, so that it will stay with you!

So let me pull the threads together. The main theme is to let each student get the most out of liberal arts training without the fetters of prelaw, premedicine, or any other kind of preprofessional studies, except to the extent that such requirements may be absolutely indispensable. I would make no concessions whatever to vocationalism—there is plenty of time for that later.

In closing, permit me to check off a few words as symbols of the various components of the thesis I have been attempting to expound: seeds, growth, inner resources; freedom, curiosity, imagination, creative powers, happiness, and fulfillment; intellectual discipline, the power to write and to speak persuasively and with lucidity; devotion to ideas and moral principles, a warm sympathy and a merciful and understanding heart; courage, integrity, steadfastness; spiritual strength and power.

Yes, these are the qualities an education in the liberal arts can foster; it is thus that alma mater should wish to nurture her sons and daughters; it is thus that a solid foundation may be laid for a career in each and every one of the professions. These are the things money can't buy.

An Illustration: The Anthony Cramer Treason Case

My old friend, Professor Elliott Cheatham, suggested the title of the second part. "Why don't you try to prove your points by means of a concrete example," he said.

"How?" I replied.

And his answer was, "By telling the story of the Anthony Cramer case."

And so I shall tell you about the most thrilling experience of my professional life. In that case, in the midst of World War II, as assigned counsel for an indigent defendant, I successfully defended a German-born American citizen who had dealings with the saboteurs who came in submarines from Germany and landed in Florida and Long Island. It was the first treason case to reach the Supreme Court in the history of the United States.

At midnight of June 13, 1942, a group of German saboteurs, who had gone through the rigors of an intensive course of training in the use of explosives, secret writing, and the location of the nerve centers of manufacturing plants, railroads, and means of communication, landed from a German submarine on the beach near Amagansett, Long Island, where they buried in the sand a large quantity of TNT, time clocks, fuses, detonators, pencil bombs, delayed action bombs, and other equipment to be used in carrying out their mission of destruction. At about the same time another similar group landed at Ponte Vedra Beach in Florida. Within a few days the FBI had every one of these men in custody. What promised to be a deadly plan of wholesale sabotage, intended to paralyze the American war effort, was nipped in the bud. All this was done in secrecy and without any knowledge at the time by the American public.

One day in August, 1942, I had played a round of golf at Westhampton, Long Island, and had returned to my summer home there. As I was sitting on the terrace with Mrs. Medina in a very comfortable frame of mind, the telephone rang. It was Judge John C. Knox of the United States District Court for the Southern District of New York, then the senior judge of the district. He was an old friend of mine, and he proceeded to tell me that he had something he wanted me to do. Without any hesitation I said, "John, whatever it is, the answer is yes."

"You'd better wait till I tell you what it is; for it is very serious business." And he then told me very briefly about the landing of the saboteurs and their capture and said that there was in custody and under indictment for treason, because of some dealings with these saboteurs, a man named Anthony Cramer, who was a humble worker, then employed on the night shift in the boiler room of a small manufacturing plant in Brooklyn. He told me that Cramer was wholly without means to hire any lawyer, that it was important to demonstrate to the American people and to the world that, under our system of American justice, the poor man is just as much entitled to the advice of competent counsel as is a man with plenty of money. He explained that he wanted me to defend the accused as a patriotic duty.

Of course I accepted, and the next day I had an interview with Cramer in a little room in the basement of the courthouse where I now function as a judge. The door had the usual bars one finds in a place of confinement and we were locked in together. There was a little basin with running water in one corner. The prisoner proceeded to tell me his story.

In substance his story was that over the years he had become friendly with another German named Werner Thiel; they had worked together in some of the automobile factories and they were buddies. While out somewhere in the Middle West Cramer had become an American citizen, but Thiel had not. In 1934 or 1935 they both joined the Friends of New Germany in Hammond, Indiana, for recreation, but Cramer subsequently dropped out. When the Bund activities started

Thiel joined but Cramer did not. Thiel enjoyed the drilling and all the other Bundist activities. When the war came Thiel went back to Germany by way of Japan.

On the morning of June 22, 1942, Cramer was in his room just getting into bed, as he worked on a night shift, when a strange voice called his name from the hall of the rooming house where he lived. He paid no attention to this, whereupon an unsigned note in an unknown handwriting was slipped under his door. It read: "Be at the Grand Central Station tonight at eight o'clock, the upper platform near the information booth, Franz from Chicago has come into town and wants to see you; don't fail to be there."

Cramer said he knew no one by the name of Franz, that his first thought was to disregard the note, but his curiosity got the best of him and he went down to Grand Central Station. After he had waited around about ten minutes Thiel appeared. Cramer said that he made no inquiry as to the mysterious method of getting in touch with him, but one of the first things he said to Thiel was, "Say, how have you come over, have you come by submarine?"

Thiel looked startled, smiled, and said, according to Cramer, "Some other time I am going to tell you all about this."

The upshot was that Thiel told Cramer that he was to remember that Thiel was anti-Nazi and that his name was now Bill Thomas, and he showed Cramer a draft card bearing the name of "William Thomas." Thiel asked Cramer about his fiancée, Norma Kopp, who worked as a domestic servant in Westport, Connecticut, and Cramer suggested that he write to Norma and ask her to come to New York.

There were two or three meetings with Thiel and with Thiel and a man named Kerling, who had landed from one of the submarines, at the Twin Oaks Inn and at Thompson's Cafeteria near the Grand Central Station; and, after the last of these meetings, Thiel went to the washroom of the Twin Oaks

Inn, took off his money belt, which included $3,670 in United States currency, including some ten dollar gold notes and a number of two dollar bills, both of which had long been out of circulation. Cramer took the money belt, went to his room, and later put the money in a small safe deposit box he had previously used when he owned a few shares of stock, which he had bought for four hundred or five hundred dollars and subsequently sold. In the safe deposit box Cramer carefully placed in a separate pile two hundred dollars which was the amount which Thiel had previously borrowed from him before going back to Germany.

As a result of Cramer's letter to Norma Kopp she came to the city, but she never saw Werner Thiel as the FBI closed in and all the saboteurs and Cramer and Norma Kopp and the man who had pushed the note under Cramer's door were taken into custody.

After his arrest Cramer had made a number of statements to the FBI men, and he told me at this initial conference that he had foolishly tried to lie when he was first arrested by saying that Thiel's name was William Thomas and that in March, 1941, this William Thomas had gone to work in a factory on the West Coast and had not been out of the United States from that time until Cramer next saw him on June 22, 1942.

Cramer insisted that he had no inkling of the fact that these men were coming over from Germany, that he knew nothing of their mission, and that he merely suspected that Thiel had come by submarine as he could not imagine how he could have come here in any other way. He also said that he suspected that Thiel and his fellows were up to no good but that they had told him nothing about their plans.

After this long recital Cramer leaned back in his chair and said, "That isn't treason, is it?"

I replied, "I don't know." I really believe that Cramer, who had freely told all this to the FBI and signed a long statement to the same effect, had not up to that moment realized that there was a chance that he might end his life in the electric chair. His face turned a sort of greenish white color, he even swayed a bit in his chair as though he might faint, and he went over to the little basin, turned on the faucet, and threw the cold water over his face and head for a few minutes.

The next thing I did was to organize a staff of defense counsel. An old friend, John McKim Minton, who had a good deal of trial experience in criminal cases, agreed to join and so did John W. Jordan, an associate of my law firm, with whom for many years I had been in the habit of working on legal questions and the writing of briefs. Later another one of my associates, Richard Talliesyn Davis, worked extensively and most effectively on the case. Judge Knox amplified his original order appointing me as assigned counsel by including the names of the others.

We then got to work. Cramer was incarcerated in the Federal House of Detention on West Street in New York City, and I went up there to get further details and to fill in his background, which was that of an agricultural worker in Ollendorf, Westphalia, Germany, where he had served for a week or ten days in the German army in the last days of the first World War, just before the Armistice. A German farmer in Iowa had paid his passage to this country in 1925; and the rest of his history was that of a humble worker who drifted restlessly from one type of work to another, but who had never been discharged for cause by an employer nor had he been in trouble of any kind with the authorities. Anyway, as I started to talk to him in the House of Detention a number of guards surrounded us. I refused to interview my client under these circumstances, but their orders were explicit. So I went back to Judge Knox and straightened that out. This man was my client and he was going to get everything that my knowledge of the law and my strength could give him. The Constitution guarantees a defendant in a criminal case a right to counsel; and this does not mean the services of a lawyer with whom a defendant may confer only with guards standing around listening to everything that is said.

The task of preparation was a most arduous one; but we followed every lead we could and I do not think that any factual surprises were sprung on us at the trial. It was evident that Norma Kopp would be one of the principal witnesses against us; and I insisted upon the production by the FBI of everything that had been found in Cramer's room. He had made no effort to hide anything, and it turned out that most of the evidence produced against him at the trial was connected in one way or another with letters and other papers and articles found in his room. One of the strongest points we made throughout the trial was that he never showed the slightest consciousness of guilt.

The most difficult part of the case very naturally had to do with the law. Strange as it may seem, no treason conviction had ever been reviewed by the Supreme Court in the whole history of the Republic. There was a vast background of English law; there were a few lower federal court cases arising during the War of 1812; there was one rather ambiguous case which had arisen during the Civil War, but most of the treason charges during the Civil War had been disposed of by military commissions. Of course, we had the minutes of the Constitutional Convention at which the treason article of the Constitution was drafted, but the references were few and not too helpful. It became necessary to go through a huge mass of Colonial documents, early state constitutions, miscellaneous literature, and whatever memoirs and diaries of the time we could dig out.

Perhaps you will think that some time during this long process of preparation for trial our interest and our industry might have flagged. But they did not, and I can honestly say that I worked harder on that case than I did on any other in my whole professional experience.

One reason for this perhaps was that after I had undertaken

Cramer's defense I noticed that people generally and my friends in particular, especially the wives, began to treat me with a certain coolness. It was hardly perceptible at first. But then I heard one or two of these *sotto voce* remarks, which were probably intended for my hearing, to the effect that, "Of course, Harold Medina isn't doing all this for nothing" and other slurs and little hints. When we actually got on trial this hostile attitude became more pronounced. None of my friends ever said anything to me directly about it. Nor were there any disparaging comments in any of the newspapers. They naturally played up the government side throughout, however, and no one would have suspected that I had undertaken the defense of Cramer as a patriotic duty. The general public which thronged in the courtroom every day of the trial indicated to us very plainly that they thought perhaps we were in some way involved.

It was very natural that the courtroom should be crowded every day with hostile spectators. The very atmosphere seemed charged with bitterness. On one occasion when Mrs. Minton, the wife of my principal associate, was in court she overheard a conversation between two men who were seated near her. "Who's that fellow with the black mustache?" asked one of them, referring to me. In those days I really had a black mustache and it was long enough for me to get hold of the ends and give them a tug once in a while. "Oh, he represents the German government," answered the other.

After a recess one day I was walking up the aisle of the courtroom to the counsel table when a spectator stood up and spat in my face. I think this is the worst thing that ever happened to me in my whole life. Fortunately, as the result of many years of trial work, I had developed a certain self-control and I instantly realized that any sort of dispute or fracas could only be detrimental to my client; and so I wiped off my face with my handkerchief, returned to the counsel table, and said nothing to anyone about it, at the time.

54

The Treason Article of the Constitution, which is Article III, Section 3, reads in part:

Treason against the United States shall consist only in levying War against them, or in adhering to their Enemies, giving them Aid and Comfort. No person shall be convicted of Treason unless on the Testimony of two Witnesses to the same overt Act, or on Confession in open Court.

The statute implementing this constitutional provision, 18 United States Code, Section 2381, reads:

Whoever, owing allegiance to the United States, levies war against them or adheres to their enemies, giving them aid and comfort within the United States or elsewhere, is guilty of treason.

Our law points centered about what constituted an overt act of treason and the application of the two-witness rule. The indictment had charged ten overt acts, including Cramer's meeting in restaurants with Thiel and Kerling, the conceal-ment of the money and the money belt, the writing of the letter to Norma Kopp, and the false statements made by Cramer to the FBI after his arrest.

At the close of the government's case I made a series of motions to dismiss the indictment and severally to dismiss the charges relative to each and every one of the alleged overt acts on the ground that none of them constituted an overt act of treason within the meaning of the Constitution and the statute and also on the ground that they were not supported by proof by the necessary two witnesses. These motions were summarily denied.

And so I was faced with the question of whether or not we should put Cramer on the witness stand in his own defense. We felt sure of his innocence. He was ready to tell everything, just as he had told it to me in that little room in the basement of the courthouse months before. But might not he thus, with his own testimony, be held to be one of the two witnesses required by the law? No one could answer this. The answer could only be given by the nine men sitting on the Supreme Court. I felt that any rational interpretation could scarcely include him as one of the two witnesses, and that the "confession in open court" must mean a confession of guilt and not a protestation of innocence such as Cramer was about to make. But it was a fateful decision and I asked the trial judge to declare a recess and permit me to discuss the matter with my client in private. So we were taken back to the same little room in the basement of the courthouse and there, for an hour or more, we struggled to make the right decision. After I had explained all the possibilities to him he still insisted that he was innocent and that he wanted the opportunity to face his accuser. Think of it! This poor fellow, with practically no education except such as he gave himself, no background, no friends, weighing the pros and cons and then having the spirit to tell me that he not only was ready to face the music but that he would do so unless I positively forbade it. And so we decided to put him on the stand; and I have felt from that day to this that, despite a grueling cross-examination and the threat of the electric chair, he never lied once. I know the United States attorney took a different view, but that is his business.

I worked all night on my summation. I often did that in important criminal cases. Instead of wearing one down it works one up to a certain pitch of nervous intensity, which seems to make ideas and the words flow more easily.

I thought and still think Cramer was innocent, that he never entertained any treasonable intent against the United States. But the government had made the most of every scrap of evidence that could be used against him. There were certain letters he had written to Thiel and to his family before Pearl Harbor, which had been intercepted and preserved. There was another letter, written on April 21, 1942, to a friend in

Chicago with whom Cramer and Thiel had at one time been associated in a delicatessen business in Florida which had failed. On cross-examination every effort had been made to make Cramer seem evasive, despite the fact that he had admitted every last detail of what he had done. And this effort had succeeded in eliciting a claim by Cramer that the translations of his letters were in some particulars inaccurate. He had not been quick-witted enough to sense the significance of my admission that the translations were correct. Although his long written statement to the FBI and the testimony of his principal interrogator had contained no such statement, one of the FBI men testified that Cramer had told him in private that Thiel had told him that he was in the United States on a mission for the German government. Norma Kopp had given damaging testimony, but with a strong motive to keep herself out of the clutches of the law by helping to convict Cramer. The mass of detail required the most skillful handling.

The principal obstacle was to get the jury to understand a man like Cramer, whom the prosecutor very naturally portrayed as unscrupulous and cunning and possessed of a deepseated antipathy to the United States. But his whole life proved the contrary, as it seemed to me. I had eliminated every prospective woman juror by showing some prejudice or by the use of peremptory challenges, as I remembered the reaction to me on the part of the wives of my friends, which I have already mentioned; and I told those twelve men frankly that their most difficult task would be to try to understand Cramer and put themselves in his place, with his background and all the petty circumstances of his life. He was one of those hard-working plodders who had never got anywhere. His whole existence had been drab and colorless. Work, work, work, with absolutely nothing to show for it; but because of his meager savings and his economical ways he was never destitute or in want, never on relief.

He had tried and tried to improve his English. In his room

was a pamphlet entitled, "How to Improve Your English," with the pages so worn by constant use that it was practically falling apart. When in Indiana he had studied nights for five long years to pass the examination for the position of stationary engineer. But the certificate he received was not recognized in New York and he had to do the work all over again.

In his letter to Thiel of November 25, 1941, he told Thiel that he had declined a $100-a-week job in Detroit "as I do not want to soil my hands with war work," and he added, "Not vocabularies, but defiance, boldness, will, and sharp weapons will decide the war and the German Army and the German people are not lacking in these." In another letter, dated in April, 1942, addressed to the friend in Chicago whom I have already mentioned, he said, referring to the possibility of his being drafted, "Personally I should not care at all to be misused by the American Army as a world conqueror." To his family in Germany he wrote on December 3, 1941, of "the gigantic sacrifices which the glorious disciplined German army is making from day to day for the homeland," that "every day here I hear the shrieks of hatred and the clamor for annihilation from the hostile foreigners," and that a lost war "means today a complete extirpation of the German nation."

I think, if some day you should read what I said about these letters in my summation you would be proud to see what an American lawyer has a right and is under a duty to say about free speech in an American courtroom. Cramer had a right to say the things he wrote in these letters. We are not mere pawns in a game to be shunted around by those who govern our country. Cramer's letters to Thiel and to his family were written before Pearl Harbor. Cramer had a right to say that he was opposed to the war, that he did not want to dirty his hands with war material, and that he had a high opinion of the German army. Moreover he was then in his forties, and, after

58

the United States entered the war, he had the right to say that he disliked military service. He was not the only American who disliked the idea of being drafted. We may not like such statements or the people who make them, but that is beside the point.

After the summations and in that awesome moment before giving his instructions to the jury, in a case which involved the death penalty, Judge Henry W. Goddard, later one of my brothers as a United States District judge, but who has since died, beckoned to me to rise, which I did. He then proceeded to praise me and my associates for our work in defending Cramer as assigned counsel without compensation.

What was I to do? I had made up my mind from the beginning that not one word should come from my lips to give the jury the impression that I was anything other than a lawyer retained by Cramer to defend him. He was entitled to the best defense we could give him. He was entitled to the full advantage of everything which went with the fact that I was there standing by his side as his lawyer. Nor did I want the jury to think for even one moment that perhaps I thought Cramer was guilty, but was defending him only because I had been assigned by the court to do it. And I could not help reflecting that perhaps the judge had chosen this particular time in order to soften or tone down the effect of my summation on the jury. It is more than likely that I did Judge Goddard an injustice by even permitting such a thought to cross my mind. But it did, and so I said:

> May it please your Honor, I have a most distressing and disagreeable task, and that is to object to the fact that you have mentioned that to this jury, and to take exception to your Honor's comment. It is something I do with the most extreme regret, but I honestly feel that my duty requires that I do it. I do not think the jury should have been told

that. I have tried to keep it from them myself, and I have not mentioned it.

Can you imagine how difficult it was for me to say those words? Here was a judge whom I honored and revered; to hurt him, to do what might seem to him to be twisting his words of thanks and appreciation into conduct detrimental to our defense of Cramer, to do what would probably seem to him to be a contemptible thing! But I had to do it, if I was to remain true to my trust.

The jury were out for several hours. It was obvious that they were giving the case the most careful consideration. They returned to the courtroom and had the entire testimony of Norma Kopp read over to them by the court reporters, but in the end they brought forth a verdict of guilty.

For a man charged with a crime punishable by death, the time of the bringing in of such a verdict is one of life's darkest moments. But you will remember what I said yesterday about humanity and that warm and sympathetic understanding which one man has for another. Well, instead of feeling resentful or blaming me, as in their agony most persons under such circumstances would do, Cramer came up to me and put his arm around my shoulder and begged me to be sure to get the forty-five dollars that was coming to him for the last week he had worked in the factory in Brooklyn. He was thankful for all I had done for his defense and wanted me to take the last cent he had in the world as that was all he could do.

But I said, "No, Tony, you will need that money to buy tobacco or something or other in jail. But I appreciate what you have just said and I am sorry we lost."

After a few days Cramer stood before Judge Goddard for sentence. Naturally, the hue and cry in the newspapers and elsewhere was for the death sentence. The whole affair had filled people with fear that we might be surrounded on all sides with spies and saboteurs secretly smuggled into the country. The demand was for Cramer's life as an example to others of German birth and with German sympathies who might be tempted to give assistance to other saboteurs coming here for similar purposes.

How I fought for that man's life that day! I pointed out that no one pretended that he had any advance knowledge that these saboteurs were coming, that no one pretended that he had any knowledge of their plans. No testimony had been introduced by the government to warrant any such inferences. I went over his background and what he had done and the frankness with which he had revealed everything to the FBI, after his first false statements; and I emphasized every possible mitigating circumstance that I could think of. Finally, after we had argued back and forth for some little time, I concluded by telling Judge Goddard that my work was done, and that the decision now lay between him and his conscience. The result was a term of imprisonment for forty-five years, with a statement that the judge would recommend that he be not paroled, and a fine of $10,000.

We then appealed to my present court, then known as the United States Circuit Court of Appeals for the 2nd circuit. But we lost there and the court in its opinion rejected our arguments relating to the admission of certain evidence which we claimed was prejudicial and improper, and held that the term "overt act" in the Constitution and the statute was to be construed as no different from an overt act in an ordinary conspiracy case.

By this time much of the public clamor had subsided and the hostility which I had observed in the social circles in which I move seemed to have disappeared.

We made an application to the Supreme Court for certiorari which was promptly granted. We were ultimately given No. 13 on the calendar, which made a distinctly unfavorable impression upon Cramer who was then in prison in Atlanta. But I always liked No. 13. When the USJ New York license plates were first issued I got USJ-13. Governor Dewey's executive secretary called me up to explain that it just came out that way according to priority, but I said I was really pleased and wouldn't have it changed.

As soon as the Supreme Court took the case I noted a distinctly more favorable attitude of the public generally toward myself and my associates. People were beginning at last to realize that it was absurd to suppose that we were being paid anything to defend Cramer and it was equally absurd to suppose that we could be in any way associated with what he had done.

The preparation of the briefs in the Supreme Court was again an arduous task. We literally combed the principal libraries of the country to find material casting light on the proper meaning and interpretation of the treason article, but we still relied on the reasoning of certain of the English cases and the early American cases, distinguishing some and quoting from others. This proved to be a mistake, as I shall tell you later.

As I always did, before the argument of a case in the Supreme Court, I went down to Washington about a week in advance and spent the time in the Library of Congress studying such materials as were available, which were extensive, and working up my oral argument. The Court had set aside an entire day, lacking a few minutes, to hear arguments on the case; and as the Solicitor General and I and our assistants went up to the counsel table, the courtroom was almost deserted. I verily believe that on that day I made the best appellate argument I ever made in my life. After a time people began to drift in and pretty soon the courtroom was comfortably filled. There was a barrage of questions from the bench, and I wondered how I could get them to stop the questions and let me develop my argument. Finally, when two or three of the justices asked questions at the same time, I held up my arm as if to defend myself and said, "One at a time, please." After that they left me alone.

At that stage I think the best I felt that I could hope for was a new trial. The evidence points were really good. One of them had to do with a copy of the Constitution which had been printed in an issue of the New York *Times* dated September 17, 1937, and Cramer had this in his room. He had evidently read it over and over and he had underlined a number of different clauses which puzzled him, references to habeas corpus, ex post facto laws, bills of attainder, letters of marque and reprisal, and so on. Another one he had underlined was the entire treason article. Possibly some of my readers recall that the Constitution provides in the concluding paragraph of the treason section: "The Congress shall have Power to declare the Punishment of Treason, but no Attainder of Treason shall work Corruption of Blood, or Forfeiture except during the Life of the Person attainted." This copy of the Constitution, with the parts underlined by Cramer, was supposed to show that Cramer harbored a treasonable intent toward the United States. This was a preposterous claim, but the prosecutor made much of it. It was obviously damaging to Cramer, and I thought I might get a new trial because of this alleged error.

The other evidence point on which I particularly relied had to do with the fact that at the beginning of the trial the government produced one of the Germans who had been on one of the submarines. And he proceeded to describe with greatest detail how these saboteurs were trained in Germany and to describe all the TNT and bombs and other incendiary devices, which were brought into the courtroom as exhibits. I told the trial judge that a certain amount of this was perhaps necessary in order to show the plan and what these saboteurs were here for, but I had conceded in my opening to the jury that the men had come for purposes of sabotage; and I most earnestly pleaded that an hour or so of that kind of testimony was enough and that if this witness were permitted to continue hour after hour to describe the gruesome details of the enterprise and the detonators and bombs and other articles were handed around and shown to the jury, the whole effect would be to create such a feeling of fear on the part of the jurors that it would be absolutely impossible thereafter for Cramer to get a fair trial.

Anyway, after several months, the Supreme Court handed down a memorandum which gave me hope for final and complete victory. They set the case down for further argument and they specified the points we were to argue. Even a cursory examination of these points, which had to do with my fundamental contentions relative to the nature of an overt act of treason and the application of the two-witness rule, was enough to satisfy me that the Court was probably equally divided and that we had at least fair chance of persuading a fifth judge, necessary for a majority, on one of our underlying theories.

I may say parenthetically that at the close of the entire case at the trial I amplified my motions and made them in such a crisscross manner as to raise substantially every question of law which possibly could be raised as to the sufficiency of the evidence to sustain the whole charge or any part of the charge. This strategy led to an important concession on the part of the government. You know how prosecutors are. They never like to have defense counsel get his foot in the door even the tiniest bit. They would rather make concessions which they believe to be unimportant rather than to have a trial judge rule in favor of the defendant on any single phase of the case. It is a curious bit of psychology. However this may be, as a result of my motions, the United States attorney withdrew and consented to the dismissal of all the overt acts except the two relating to meetings in taverns or restaurants and the last which had to do with the false statements made by Cramer to the FBI at the time of his first interview with the FBI agents after his arrest. So, in the Supreme Court, we only had these three overt acts to deal with.

The new complexion of affairs, after the case was set down for further argument, led to a fundamental change of policy. This illustrates one of the things we lawyers should often do but seldom have the courage to do. We abandoned the English cases, threw out the earlier American lower court decisions which followed the War of 1812, and proceeded to further develop our own theory of the meaning of the constitutional and statutory provisions, without all the confusion attendant upon the discussion of a large number of cases, with distinctions, and the quotation of paragraphs or phrases here and there, and so on. I need not add that this may be all very well in a court of last resort which has not previously ruled on the question, but it is a dangerous business to do in an intermediate appellate court. Anyway, it was a bold move and we only adopted this strategy after a long conference between Mr. Minton, Mr. Davis, and myself.

What it boiled down to was that all the government had shown with reference to the meetings in the taverns or restaurants was that Cramer and the saboteurs, Thiel and Kerling, were seen together. Not a single one of the FBI men had heard what was said by any of the men sitting at the table and Cramer had not even paid for the beer. I argued, in substance, that the whole background of the English history of treason and that of the framers of our Constitution was such as to produce in the minds of those who composed the phraseology of the constitutional definition of treason an attitude of utter hostility to the conviction of any person for treason except under the clearest possible circumstances. It is the only crime defined in the Constitution. An indifferent act, such as walking across the street or sitting down at a table, had no connotation whatever of treasonable action.

The second argument in the Supreme Court was very exciting. The courtroom was crowded, with extra seats provided all along the sides. The wives of some of the justices were there, many members of the diplomatic corps, and other distinguished persons. Quite a contrast to the empty courtroom we had as we started the first argument months before.

In the end we prevailed by a five-to-four vote, and Mr. Justice Jackson writing for the court stated (325 U.S. 1, 37):

> It appeared upon the trial that at all times involved in these acts Kerling and Thiel were under surveillance of the Federal Bureau of Investigation. By direct testimony of two or more agents it was established that Cramer met Thiel and Kerling on the occasions and at the places charged and that they drank together and engaged long and earnestly in conversation. This is the sum of the overt acts as established by the testimony of two witnesses. There is no two-witness proof of what they said nor in what language they conversed. There is no showing that Cramer gave them any information whatever of value to their mission or indeed that he had any to give. No effort at secrecy is shown, for they met in public places. Cramer furnished them no shelter, nothing that can be called sustenance or supplies, and there is no evidence that he gave them encouragement or counsel, or even paid for their drinks.

Having thus held that the evidence was insufficient to support a finding that Cramer had given aid and comfort to the enemy as charged in overt acts one and two, the Court reversed without passing on the sufficiency of the evidence to support overt act ten; and it was not even clear that a retrial was contemplated.

Our final task was to avoid the possibility of a new trial relative to overt act ten and to negotiate the best arrangement we could for the prosecution of Cramer on a less serious charge under the Trading with the Enemy Act. This was done, Cramer pleaded guilty, and he was then sentenced to prison for a term of six years, which, with time off for good behavior, was completed in four.

During the time Cramer was serving the sentence he was in the Federal penitentiary at Atlanta, Georgia. I had been made a United States District judge and was engaged in the trial of the Communist leaders. This made Cramer a very prominent citizen in the penitentiary. He wrote to me on one occasion saying that he and his fellow prisoners could hardly wait to get the newspapers and see how I was doing. And, he concluded, as I shall now conclude, by telling me that I was the most popular Federal judge in the Atlanta penitentiary.

6 A Liberal Education and the Advancement of American Freedom

1955

What I shall say here represents no more than the meditations of one who, trained in the beginning as a humanist, has had the sort of everyday experiences which most lawyers and judges meet in the course of a busy, active life. In other words, I am not a philosopher, although I wish I were. But a lot of ideas on the relationship between freedom and a liberal education have been running around in the back of my head for some little time, and I welcome this opportunity to set them down.

By way of preliminary, I shall sketch a bit of background. When I was a freshman at Princeton it became plain to me that I was very definitely a nonconformist. All the freshmen had to wear little black caps, corduroy trousers, and other parts of an identical outfit; and we were all supposed to look alike and do the same things. I need not tell you that my nonconformity got me into a lot of trouble; and that sort of thing has been going on ever since. I was the first man in the class, for instance, to wear a mustache and many efforts were made to remove it, in one way or another; without success, however, I am happy to say.

A demand for conformity, stemming from the herd instinct of the human race has probably been going on since long before the time of the Egyptians. The emotional force behind it is fear. Consequently, in a period of crisis and rapid social change and adjustment the demand for conformity becomes more and more insistent. This sort of thing seems to operate in cycles. Naturally enough with the scientific developments and discoveries of recent years and the violent changes which necessarily follow the destructive and disintegrating forces of a great world war, we find ourselves today in one of these recurrent periods when, because of the intuitive and often unrealized fear of what the future may hold in store, the demand is widespread and powerful. Paradoxically enough, it is precisely in such critical times that it is most important to think clearly and avoid panicky ill-conceived decisions. And we must remember that all life is a dichotomy, an unending series of choices between this and that.

Again by way of background, and largely but not wholly due to the deliberate efforts of our Communist friends, the word "liberal" has taken on a sinister and evil connotation. The word seems almost to be taboo in polite society, as though a liberal, while perhaps not an out-and-out Communist, were at least a "parlor pink" or a "fellow traveler," perhaps a bit inclined to be subversive if the opportunity presented itself and anyway a nasty, disagreeable sort of fellow.

Frankly I resent all this. I was brought up to think that just about the best kind of a person to be or to be with was an honest-to-goodness liberal. I do not intend to be frightened away because the Communists and their coadjutors have tried to appropriate the word "liberal" just as they have the names of our great presidents, Abraham Lincoln and Thomas Jefferson, by the use of Aesopian language twisting names and personalities to suit their purposes. I know just how they do it too. When I presided over that trial of the eleven Communist leaders in 1949, at first I was puzzled by all their constant talk about democracy and freedom, always of the Russian variety. It suddenly dawned on me that this was simply a clever piece of propaganda to make Marxism-Leninism more palatable to the American public. That is how the Communists became liberals. And don't forget that the word liberal fundamentally means free.

But I do not care about the Communists at the moment. Let them do as they please, and the politicians too, who seem inclined to call themselves liberals when it serves their purposes. I consider myself a liberal, I should like to have you think of me as a liberal, and I hope I shall remain a liberal for the rest of my life.

Well, what is a liberal anyway? This may have some bearing upon what we mean by a liberal education. And so I shall give you a few definitions of my own, so that you may intelligently follow what I have to say.

In defining the terms "liberal," "conservative," "reactionary," and "radical," dictionary meanings are of little assistance. These words have been so variously used in different contexts that it seems that the only generalization which can fairly be made respecting them is that the shades of meaning attributable to them are, in large measure, personal to the definer. For this reason, it is probably more useful and certainly more accurate to discuss these words in terms of their connotation.

To my personal way of thinking, a liberal man must be a thinking man, one who has learned to evaluate his experience and the world about him independently and freely, using the ideas of others only as the starting points of his own analysis and creativity. But this alone does not complete the picture. The liberal not only has his own concepts of right or wrong, desirable and undesirable, and so forth, but he is always prepared to accept criticism and to try to understand opposing views. He constantly stands ready and is anxious to reappraise his own conclusions, ideas, and concepts of truth in light of differing theories and new information available to him.

Just by way of footnote here, I should like to remind you that this is precisely the way the Communists talk. But woe to the individual who fails to follow to the letter the official Communist line of the moment. He is forthwith excluded from the ranks of the elect. This is just an example of their double talk.

The conservative differs from the liberal particularly in his reluctance to revise original estimates. He is not wholly without an inquiring mind and capacity for change but he instinctively struggles against espousing new ideas and rejecting preexisting notions of truth. In any appraisal in which he might engage, he seems to bestow a quality of good upon that which exists or is current merely because it happens to be the prevalent practice or view right now. As a consequence, a much more persuasive argument must be directed at him to induce any change or revision of the current norm. He is basically a follower in the day-to-day journal of progress and seems to rely more upon the support of general social acceptance than upon faith in the strength of his own convictions independently arrived at.

The reactionary is one who not only resists change but actively combats any deviation from the status quo. To this man, there is no reappraisal of existing ideas or concepts, but instead, an utter unwillingness to consider, much less accept, the merit or worthiness of any view differing from his own. Within the framework of the reactionary philosophy, change is inherently undesirable and reason plays little, if any, part in any appraisal of existing phenomena or new ideas. His is a static and perhaps even retrogressive concept of life and society; his world is one composed of what has been and never of what will be or should be.

The radical is markedly similar to the reactionary in his fanatic devotion to his own belief and his unwillingness to accept or tolerate the views of others. However, where the reactionary decries change, the radical can see no merit in

71

anything but violent deviation from traditional concepts or ideas. Rather than engaging in reasoned reëxamination of prevailing views, the radical proceeds on the assumption that there is a positive quality in change merely for the sake of change and, correlatively, that the more emphatic the deviation from existing ideas, the more desirable the change. As is the case with the typical reactionary, the thought process of the radical is more often emotional than rational, and in dealing with this kind of mentality one encounters a signal intolerance for the views of others.

So much for background.

If we are to discuss the relationship between a liberal education on the one hand and the advancement of American freedom on the other, it is important that we should have some pretty clear notion of what a liberal education is and what we mean by freedom. Unfortunately these words have been so frequently bandied about that practically everyone takes them for granted; and the average citizen goes on his merry way really without having the slightest notion of what they mean. It would be a barren task were I to attempt to sketch the history of the education of free men from the time of the great cathedral schools and universities of the Middle Ages and the Renaissance, with a description of the trivium and the quadrivium and the various ways in which, over the centuries, man sought ever-increasing accretions to his knowledge of man and of the cosmos. It seems better to take stock of what are commonly accepted as the purposes and ends of a liberal education.

In the first place I think we will all agree that at the very top of the list comes training in the use of our minds.

In the second place it is the function of a liberal education to fill its votaries with a burning zeal for the ascertainment of truth, the whole truth, no matter where it leads or whom it hurts. Imbued with this spirit and determination, the seeker

72

after truth soon finds the search unending. We go on and on, ever seeking to scale the heights and open up new vistas.

Without this ferment of curiosity and this indomitable will to know, how can there be freedom?

The third great primary object of a liberal education is more elusive, more difficult to define, and yet perhaps fully as important as the others. For, as we have said, one of the functions of a liberal education is to develop our inner resources so that each of us will find himself a satisfactory person with whom to live. Must we always be dependent upon the company of friends or acquaintances?

Let me ask each of you this question: What voices speak to you, my friend? Are they from within; or are they alien voices, not yours but those of someone else or of the world at large, guiding you hither and thither in the mist?

I wonder, too, if it is not a matter of prime importance that we form some warm and sympathetic notion of the dignity of man. If we do this will we not of necessity become more tolerant of the views of others and of their little whimsies or even of their sins? Good will is one of the most precious spiritual forces in existence. Will we not be happier, more useful men and women, if subjection to the educational process of a liberal education trains us naturally to a love of our fellow man?

Even in the bringing up of children how important it is to realize that each little soul is the master of its own destiny, and that steering each into the ways we think are best may occasionally be no more than the manifestation of our own egotism, to the detriment of the very person whom we are so eager to assist. I have often seen the careers of young men all but ruined because a father or grandfather pushed into the law someone destined to be a poet or a musician or a businessman or a philosopher.

Now, the wonderful thing about this sort of liberal education is that it is so flexible. Over this great land of ours there are literally hundreds of colleges which, free from state control or domination of any sort from without, pursue this quest in their several, separate ways. In some, mathematics is required right up through senior year. In others, a majority of the students take Latin throughout their full course. Despite all the clacking of the utilitarians, Greek is far from dead. Here and there the natural and applied sciences take precedence. In not a few the emphasis is on sociology, anthropology, and psychology. And in all these liberal arts colleges we find an increasing interest in spiritual forces, in religion, and sound principles of morality. There is a pattern of no pattern. And I ask you if this is not a healthy sign that the education of free men and women in America is in good hands.

How about freedom? What is freedom anyway? Well, to me freedom is a state of mind; it is a way of life. It is a concept, an idea as slippery as an icy slope on a cold day, and as changing as the iridescent throat of a peacock. From one viewpoint it is the individual on the one hand, and all the powers of government and the state and society on the other. How much individual freedom is consistent with the needs of a given nation or community at a given time? Freedom is the opposite of slavery; there is physical freedom and the freedom of the mind. Freedom is more precious than all the gold and all the jewels of the Indies. But it is not static; it is subject to the inexorable laws of growth and decay.

Not so long ago Mrs. Medina and I had an exciting experience on Edward R. Murrow's *Person to Person* television program. Frankly I didn't know what we were in for. I thought it was all going to be rehearsed in advance. Oh, no, nothing like that. This man Murrow is a remarkable man. One of the questions he popped at me, out of the blue, was: "Judge, can you recommend some little book, of a hundred pages or so, which will explain all about this freedom business?" Well, I nearly fell off my chair. Freedom is the study of a lifetime. Our Bill of Rights, which looks so simple when we first read it in school, is a dynamic, flexible, ever-expanding, and growing definition of our fundamental rights. Like the search for truth the ultimate in freedom is always just over the horizon, just beyond our grasp. The trick is not to lose it or any part of it, but rather to get as much more of it as we can properly assimilate.

And yet the temper of the times would seem to be in the opposite direction. In our zeal to defend ourselves against the onslaughts of the Communists, we must be alert to the danger of adopting their ruthless methods and losing our freedoms in the process. It will not do merely to give lip service to these fundamental rights, as they do, whilst at the same time indulging in actions, the inevitable consequence of which must be the erosion or whittling away of our heritage of freedom.

With the complexity of modern life new problems arise. Old problems suddenly come out of the shadows and demand solution without undue delay. New chapters will be written about Freedom of Speech, Freedom of Religion, Freedom of the Press, the Equal Protection of the Laws, and all the other Freedoms so dear to our hearts. The rights of individuals must be expanded and implemented and clarified. And at the same time law observance and order must be maintained and malefactors and enemies of society justly punished. The road to freedom is a difficult road to follow, full of pitfalls and perplexities. Nothing worth while comes easily.

Let me see if I can pull the threads together. First let me add a few dabs of color to the canvas. Not so long ago I was reading the diary of John Evelyn and I came to a part where he was describing an occasion when he was taken in to see a man put to the torture. The subject was charged as a pickpocket, and the man whose pocket had been picked identified the prisoner but the prisoner refused to admit his guilt. What he saw in the torture chamber was too much for worthy John's stomach and he declined the invitation to witness what was to be done to the next victim. But there is not a word of protest in the diary. He took it for granted that this was the thing to do and it was the regular, lawful procedure.

I have another picture in my mind. John Evelyn was speaking in terms of about 1650. If we go back a century or so we will see another familiar sight. A man, often bowed with years, is chained to a stake and around his neck are hung, also in chains, the books he wrote. They are huge, bulky folios, not the sort of light literature we chiefly hear about today. And presently the fagots are lit and the man is burned to death.

Going a century the other way, in 1750 or thereabouts, we find ourselves in an attic somewhere on the left bank in Paris. Three or five or sometimes even more than ten men are writing. They are making copies of one of Voltaire's latest pamphlets. It is too risky to have them printed. But these copies go hither and yon like wildfire.

Such is conformity. These things happen when we encounter the antithesis of freedom; each of them is the product of tyranny of one kind or another. But they have all gone, blown away into oblivion by the winds of progress.

Our only hope today lies in the fostering of freedom. We must be fearless and tolerant and receptive of new ideas and new interpretations. What we all wish is more freedom. Not freedom to do as we please, to the detriment of ourselves and our neighbors, but the freedom that comes with wisdom and enlightenment. I am thankful for the liberal arts college where free men are trained to think for themselves to the glory of God and the advancement of American freedom.

7 The Liberal Arts and the Whole Man

1957

This subject, of what I think an independent liberal arts college should try to do to and for the men and women who come to it to earn their undergraduate degrees, is very dear to my heart. As I was trained in the humanistic tradition it is natural that I should use as a unifying element the ancient Greek concept of "the whole man" and I shall introduce my subject by collating a few key phrases from an article by Professor Caryl P. Haskins entitled "Science and the Whole Man." This was published in the September, 1956, proceedings of the American Academy of Arts and Sciences, one of the foremost learned societies in the United States, comparable in stature to the American Philosophical Society. Professor Haskins did not explain nor was there any occasion for him to explain to his distinguished audience of philosophers and scientists what he meant by "the whole man"; that phrase has had a definite meaning since it was coined by the Greeks centuries ago. Now comes a little part of a paragraph which is very important because this is a very closely integrated affair. He speaks of "mass standardization" as "dwarfing the individual." He speaks of "the gifted, the free, the

77

unstandardized individual" as one with "superior imagination, superior communicativeness and persuasion, superior judgment." Oh, those three—"superior imagination, superior communicativeness and persuasion"! How few of us realize as we go through life that this power to communicate thought from one person to another is so difficult! The art of persuasion is of the essence and, of course, superior judgment; I need not tell you that of all things, good judgment stands very high. He speaks of "essential non-conformity," and "essential individuality," and the critical importance in these trying times of Americans who are "independent" and "original."

But how is one to become free and independent, original and creative with "superior imagination, superior communicativeness and persuasion, superior judgment"? Surely this is a Herculean task in the midst of the demands for conformity which are becoming more and more insistent in the period of crisis and rapid social change and adjustment through which we are now passing. The human race is gregarious by instinct, and the majority, especially those in authority, always seem determined to make the rest conform to their notions of what is proper and fitting, down to the last detail. That's one little byway of our subject—conformity and non-conformity.

"Integer"—The Quality of Wholeness

Now, we're off on another tack. To students of Horace that first verse of one of his most famous poems is exceedingly difficult: "*Integer vitae scelerisque purus.*" Thousands of boys and girls have thumbed their dictionaries in vain effort to dig out the meaning of that word *integer*. It is an adjective and it means having the quality of wholeness, completeness, entireness. The general theme of what Horace was trying to tell us is that one who has this quality of wholeness in his life can face the world unafraid. But what did he mean by that? It is easy to listen to it and hear the sound, but what is the inner meaning?

Well, a person whose thumb has been cut off is not *integer*, he does not possess that quality of wholeness, because this part of his body is missing. Thus it is with any other defect.

And so, in sketching background here, I would have you notice that when we speak of a person of integrity we really mean a person who has this quality of wholeness. We shall come back to this again. Now there's another little seed—wholeness-integrity.

Just one more dab of color by way of background and I shall return to the main theme. With human beings all is growth and decay. We are never quite the same one day as the next. Everything we do or avoid doing tends to develop and strengthen our muscles and our minds and our character, or to shrivel them up and cause them to deteriorate. You remember how those fakirs over in India used to stand with one arm up in the air until it ceased for all practical purposes to be an arm.

This is an inexorable law of life, and an inexorable law of institutions too! You can't stand still. You either grow or you do the opposite of growing every day of your life. You can't get away from it. And so I say, this inexorable law of life is best expressed in the parable of the talents where there was this master who was going away on a long journey and he called in his servants and to one of them he gave five talents, and to another he gave two talents, and to a third he gave one talent, and then he went away and when he came back the servant with the five talents had speculated with them in the market or did something or other to make them reproduce another five talents, and he said: "Here, my Lord, are your five talents and another five talents that I gained by trading," and the master replied, "Oh, thou good and faithful servant, enter into the joy of thy Lord!"

You remember that, and the same thing with the man with the two talents. He went out and did some speculating and he got another two talents and then the master said the same thing to him, "Thou good and faithful servant, enter into the joy of thy Lord!" But the man with the one talent didn't want to lose it speculating so he hid it in the ground and when the master called for him, he took the one talent that he had been hiding away and he said, "Now, I give thee back thine own," and with that the master, instead of saying, "Thou good and faithful servant," said, "Thou wicked and slothful man," and then he took the one talent away from him and gave it to the man who had the ten. And I always thought when I was a boy that seemed so unfair, so wrong; why do that? And then it goes on to the part that I was going to read to you, the in-exorable law of life—this is real. There's nothing phony about this. This is what actually happens with you and with me and with everybody else every day of our lives to a greater or lesser degree. And so the parable concluded: "For unto every-one that hath shall be given, and he shall have abundance: but from him that hath not shall be taken away even that which he hath. And cast ye the unprofitable servant into outer darkness: there shall be weeping and gnashing of teeth." Now, as I said, that is the law of life-growth and decay—growth and decay! Use your talents. Develop them. Use them to the utmost and in that way you become strong. You hide them away and let them not be used—well, then the opposite.

So I say each one of us is a separate unique soul or personality. Surely the principal function of an education in the liberal arts is to help each and every one of the students to make every phase and feature of his or her personality attain its fullest development so that the result may be a harmonious, effective whole, without blemish of defect. When you once let this idea take hold, miracles are in the making. Each of us has undeveloped inner resources, capacities, and talents far beyond our hopes or dreams. The trick is how to nurture and bring them to fruition.

Now how about ways and means? We've got our objective in front of us now, haven't we? We've got two or three of these little ideas and we see the objective. Now how are you going to·do that?

Well, a person who is not free and independent cannot have the quality of wholeness. But how many of us really understand what freedom and independence mean—surely not running around doing as we please and hurting everyone else in the process. But the fact is that it is always easier to do and say just what everyone else is doing and saying. The difficulty, and what we must fight against, is the tendency of contemporary American life to run us all in a mold, to standardize us like the automobiles and the washing machines, to make us all think alike, to make us conform to the wishes of the majority of the moment, and in the end to lose that freedom and independence which are so indispensable to the man or woman of integrity. If you think and act precisely as everyone else does you are not your whole self as you should be; instead you are imitating someone else and to the extent that you are not measuring up to your own powers, you are defective and hence you have not got that quality of wholeness. A man of integrity would think and act for himself.

How is a college to approach the task of training its students

81

to think for themselves? I have heard a lot of mushy talk on the subject but I have never known anyone to produce a formula.

I remember distinctly when I first learned to think. It was in my sophomore year at Princeton, and the man who taught me was Christian Gauss, then a teacher of Romance languages and one of Woodrow Wilson's "preceptor guys," as we call them at Princeton. How he did it I shall never know. He was full of ideas and suggestions, he would guide us along and then change the subject. Everything he said seemed so tentative. He didn't seem to give a positive answer to anything. Of course, he did give some positive answers; but it didn't seem so. It was tentative, it was guiding, changing the subject and going off on tangents. And then, suddenly out of the blue one day, I realized that instead of merely repeating the thoughts of others, including the thoughts of the professors, I was thinking for myself. That man did that in some mysterious way for me and he did it for a generation of students at Princeton. A wonderful man. There are many ways of doing this. That's one. I don't have a formula. I don't know how to tell you to do it. But that is the thing you want to be after.

Now, once this initial job is done—that is, once you learn to think, and the student responds to the natural urgings of curiosity, the search for truth begins and never ends. What a joy it is to be a seeker after truth, to delve ever deeper into the secrets of the nature of man and of the universe!

Perhaps some of you will remember the words of Horace. I keep quoting him—I think of him all the time. I can repeat a half-dozen poems of Horace in Latin, verbatim without making any mistakes at all. I just love the things he has in them. Now this is one of them:

Audax omnia perpeti
gens humana ruit per vetitum nefas

"Bold to suffer every hardship, the human race rushes to its destruction in its effort to pierce the veil which hides what

82

we are forbidden to know." You wouldn't think that was written two thousand years ago, would you? But it was.

It is always difficult to find a precise English equivalent for Horatian Latin; but his meaning is crystal clear. Without this ferment of curiosity and this indomitable will to know, how can man be free? Without a mind trained and disciplined in the performance of the function of thinking, how can a person have the quality of wholeness? How easy it is—and now I'm giving you a little touch of the ways you find interference with this thinking. These are the things that prevent, that impede thinking. I've tossed them into a sentence but I don't want them to go past without your grasping them. How easy it is to be called off the scent by some wily digression; how often is our judgment betrayed by anger or by sympathy or by fear, which is enemy number one!

This brings me now to the most important part and the slipperiest. Where do religion and morals, basic principles of right and wrong, fit in? I am not discussing the Ten Commandments. I assume you will not steal or do any of the other things these Commandments forbid. Most people don't. Nor am I in the United States courthouse administering the criminal laws. I do not like to judge my fellow man. I do it when my duty compels me, otherwise I do not. Now we are talking about the fundamental human values, the road to happiness, and a sense of fulfillment of our destiny on this earth. And oh, there is another little phrase that I don't want you to miss—the fulfillment of our destiny—not our destiny in the aggregate, my destiny for me—your destiny for you. What are you put here in this world to do? Each one of us has a destiny which may or may not be fulfilled. We know that selfishness and pride and greed are responsible for most of the unhappiness and the suffering and despair. How are we to avoid all this? What have selfishness and pride to do with integrity?

Well, the whole man, the man of integrity, must be guided by some faith in a divine being and by some principles of morality or he would have a defect far more disastrous to his well-being than any of the other defects I have mentioned. We must learn how to build up spiritual strength just as we learn to build up physical strength.

Let me tell you some stories. One of the incidents of my life as an undergraduate has come back to my mind again and again, and I have never been able to explain it. For some months every Sunday afternoon someone provided me with a horse and buggy and a small green book containing a miscellaneous collection of sermons. And I would get in the buggy and go off into the back woods behind Princeton, where there were a number of small chapels. As I came to the first one I would hitch up the horse, go inside the chapel where there were perhaps three or four persons, never more than ten. There was usually one of these small foot organs—you know, the ones you pump with your feet—and somebody who could play a hymn; and we started in by singing and then I got up in the place that might be called the pulpit, a rude sort of wooden affair, and I read one of the sermons out of the book and then I led a prayer. And I got back in the buggy and went to the next chapel. And I did that for some months. I don't know who provided the horse and buggy. I can't remember who got me to do that. I can't remember why I stopped. It's a very curious thing, I have a most distinct recollection of that book. I couldn't give you the title of it or the name of it. I've tried to find it but without success. Can it be that I imagine all that? Well, of course, I don't. I know well enough that I went around with that horse and buggy all right and with that little book of sermons.

About forty years later I found myself in the midst of that trial of the Communist leaders in 1949. It was a turbulent trial and everything conceivable was done, both in and out of the courtroom, to break up the trial and to break me down. And there came that afternoon when I felt tired and faint and thought perhaps I should fall off the judge's chair and make a

84

scene, and I went out into a little anteroom and lay down on a couch. And, oh, I did some tall praying that afternoon, I tell you. You know, unless you have faith you can't pray—it doesn't mean anything. It's just no good; but I had my faith. Perhaps partly from going around with that horse and buggy. But anyway, after a little while I began to feel better and I went back on the bench that afternoon and I finished up that day, and I went through to the end of the trial.

What I am now working up to in conclusion is to tell you that the first step in our spiritual education is to realize that the most important things in life we cannot do all by ourselves. When the notion of the big "I" begins to fade out, when we realize, as I surely did in the midst of that trial, that individually we are very, very small particles in the general scheme of things, and when we turn to the true source from which we can always get strength and guidance, then and only then, are we ready and prepared to fulfill our destiny and to use to best advantage all these talents and capacities of which I have been speaking. Surely it is the function of a liberal arts college to help its students to have faith and to believe fervently in God, the High and Mighty Ruler of the universe. Surely that must be so!

And perhaps the easiest way to do this is to remember those words which form so important a part of the Communion service in my own church, which is the Episcopal Church, and they are echoed in one form or another in the services of all the other churches as well. And maybe I can give you a little background about this. You remember about the Sadducees and the Pharisees who were always making a lot of trouble for Jesus. Well, one day a lot of these Sadducees got after Him asking Him questions to put Him in a hole and He had answers that were pretty good. And, as the Bible says, He silenced the Sadducees and the multitude was astonished; and then these Pharisees ganged up on Him and they had one of them who was a lawyer, and that one who was the lawyer put the question that he thought no one could answer because he thought there wasn't any answer. They really thought they had Him with this one, and the question was: "Which is the great commandment in the Law?" They thought nobody could answer that. Now, the key to all I've been talking about is in Jesus' answer, and here it is:

> Thou shalt love the Lord thy God with all thy heart, and with all thy soul, and with all thy mind.
> This is the first and great commandment.
> And the second is like unto it, thou shalt love thy neighbor as thyself.
> On these two commandments hang all the law and the prophets.

Now I don't know whether you see through that as I do. I don't know whether you see on the one hand humility and on the other hand good will, but there they are—just as clear as though they were written in letters a thousand feet high. Those are the great dynamic spiritual forces, my friends. So hard is that lesson to learn for every one of us and yet so simple. In our daily lives, with our families, with the nation, with our foreign relations, with everything, everywhere—humility and good will.

8 Patriotism

1957

While I was in Bermuda over the Christmas holidays I spent my mornings studying Latin. I had just started Livy's *History of Rome* and was faced with the Preface, or *Praefatio*, which while difficult to translate was more than worth the effort. The days of the Roman Republic, the days of free institutions and a measure of liberty, were over and gone. Livy wrote in the time of Augustus Caesar, and centuries of Roman imperialism and tyranny lay ahead. Aloof from current problems and conspiracies Livy sat in his study, poring over such historical records as he could find, and he wrote of the heroes and happenings of the past. The theme of the *Praefatio* is that what the great men of the past said and did are important not as mere material for rhetoric and speeches, but as models for living men to follow. And so, referring to the course of events over some seven hundred years, he wrote: "You may select for yourself and for your country what you should imitate on the one hand or what you should avoid."

It is in times of danger and hysteria that freedoms are lost. What Washington and the other founders have taught us is: in the midst of crisis be steadfast and face the danger calmly.

87

And so the pattern of our liberties was laid down. Whether we like it or not, indeed, whether some of us realize it or not, the fact is that today we live in critical times; and there is grave danger that some or all of our freedoms, such as free speech, freedom of religion, the equality of all men before the law, freedom from unreasonable searches and seizures, the guarantee that our property will not be taken except by due process of law, and others may be diluted, whittled away, diminished, or even torn out of the Constitution by amendment, as with the right of a person to refuse to incriminate himself, which has been under open attack.

And so my message is to my friends and fellow members of the Sons of the Revolution, and to all the patriotic societies of America, all those deeply attached to the founders of our Republic and to the integrity of our institutions and to the principles of freedom expressed in our Bill of Rights and woven into the very fabric of our Constitution, but who seem at times more interested in parades and flag waving and the preservation of the outward apparatus and trappings than in the fundamental rights and the correlative duties without which freedom is mere illusion. In other words, we must bestir ourselves and show our love of America and our love of freedom by our thoughts and by our words and by our actions today, rather than ride along on the coattails of our great-great-great-grandfathers, with no more than lip service to the ideals and principles that lie behind those brave words of the Declaration of Independence in 1776.

This does not mean that I am unmindful of the true meaning of the Salute to the Flag or of the significance of preserving our national shrines and landmarks as reminders of our glorious past. Parades and celebrations are not only a means of keeping the fires of patriotism brightly burning; they are indispensable unless we are to forget how much we owe to those great men who made every conceivable sacrifice in order that America might be prepared to march on to her destiny.

At this point probably many of you are thinking something like this: "Don't worry about me, Judge Medina, I love freedom too; you can depend on me." But I am not so sure; let us put ourselves to the test by a few concrete examples.

Some years ago, in 1949, I was preparing to preside over the trial of the eleven leaders of the Communist conspiracy to teach and advocate the overthrow of the United States government by force and violence. You already know a good deal about the persistent and ingenious methods they used to break up that trial. By the end of August it was pretty clear that I was going to be able to carry on to the end; every strategy of turbulence, disruptive tactics, confusion, and threats had failed. Suddenly I began to read in the newspapers of a concert to be given by Paul Robeson in Peekskill under Communist auspices. I was pretty well on to them by that time and suspected this would develop into another attempt to break up the trial. And that is just what happened.

The provocative notices of the forthcoming "concert" drew immediate response from the patriotic societies. One thing led to another until the day of the "concert." The Communists and their sympathizers were there in force in buses and automobiles; there was much flag waving by the patriots and shouting and rushing around. No one knows just who was in the crowd that gathered but it soon got out of control and rocks were heaved through the windshields of some of the buses and cars; and the next morning several of the defendants in my case came into the courtroom bandaged up and the fireworks began again.

No one else, so far as I know, saw at the time or has since commented on the connection between the so-called "Peekskill Riot" and the trial. Doubtless, others realized what the Communists were up to. But I was powerless to prevent it;

my job was to preside over that case and give those defendants a fair trial according to our American traditions and standards. They had been from the first accusing me of all sorts of corruption and misdoing, including alleged connivance with the attorney general and the prosecutor. Whatever connection I was to have with that trial was going to be right in the open courtroom in plain view of all who chose to see and to listen.

But what about the patriots? After the event it was clear to all that the hue and cry in the name of patriotism was no more nor less than a foolish response to provocation designed to further the ends of the Communists. The reaction was natural enough. But we must respect the rights of others no matter how much we dislike them. These precious freedoms are not a one-way street running only in our direction, they involve correlative duties; and in just such times of excitement, which more often than we suspect are deliberately created for the occasion by the enemies of our institutions, we must insist, so far as it lies in our power as individuals to do so, that the freedoms and rights of others be strictly maintained.

Here is another story. Of course you remember the Stamp Act and the Boston Tea Party and what is described in the history books as the "Boston Massacre" in 1770. George the Third, our old friend, had sent over two British regiments— one soldier for every four Bostonians—and they were quartered in Boston. The troops paraded on the common and in the streets and their cannon faced the Assembly Building. Tension mounted. Boston increasingly resented the presence of these troops.

On Monday, March 5, 1770, the tension snapped. One Captain Goldinch, connected with one of the regiments, was crossing King Street on the way to the barracks. As the Captain passed, a barber's boy whistled through his fingers and with a curse called out that the Captain owed the barber money for dressing his hair. The Captain, exercising commendable restraint, did nothing. But a sentinel on duty by the barracks

90

gave chase and whacked the boy with the butt of his musket.

The boy's shouts woke the dead, or at least the sleeping people of Boston. A crowd gathered by the barracks, began scuffling with the soldiers on guard and pelting them with ice and snowballs. "Kill the soldier," "Kill the damn coward," "Knock him down!" The crowd cried with mounting fury. A mob formed and the sentinel backing up the steps of the Custom House shoved the rammer down his musket and primed it. To his help came seven enlisted men and a young, somewhat overanxious officer, who formed half a circle around the sentry box.

One of the soldiers struck by a missile lost his footing and fell, allowing his gun to drop from his hand. The eight soldiers, not knowing what had happened to their comrade, fired their muskets into the crowd, one after another. When the smoke cleared, five men lay sprawled on the snow—three dead, two mortally wounded.

The governor was pretty much on the spot, so the soldiers were indicted for murder; and things looked pretty bad for them.

But there was a young lawyer in Boston who was to become a member of the committee responsible for drafting the Declaration of Independence and the second president of the United States, John Adams. He is one of the great men in American history. He did not join the hue and cry. Instead, despite the fact that he had a young wife and two children and another one on the way, he undertook the defense of the soldiers, a most unpopular task as you may well imagine, and as the result of his pleading they were acquitted.

That was in 1770, but the hostility of the people to the man who defended those British soldiers was the same as the hostility I encountered when in 1942 I defended Anthony Cramer, the German-born American citizen who had been indicted for treason for certain dealings he had had with one or two of the saboteurs who had come here from Germany in submarines.

Judge Knox wanted to assign me as counsel to defend this man without compensation as a patriotic duty to demonstrate that even in the midst of war our laws were applicable to all alike without prejudice or favor, and of course I accepted the assignment.

American justice is justice for all; American liberties belong to the weak and the poor as well as to the rich and powerful, to those we detest as well as to those we love. And the test always comes when fear or emotion or prejudice brings all the forces of human psychology to bear upon our will and we are tempted to betray our heritage. The politicians are human too; when public opinion is drifting this way or that they want to get on the band wagon and get the credit. The rest of us must try our best to be open-minded and independent, to be hesitant about running with the pack, or lining ourselves up with the group that makes the most noise. How often and often the easy way turns out to be the wrong way.

If you should ask the average man in the street what is freedom, what are these American liberties people keep talking about, I think the response would be something like this: "Here we can move about as we please, without the permission of the police, and without giving any explanation to anyone of why we wish to go to California or Texas or elsewhere. Here we can find employment at the trade or profession or occupation of our choice, depending upon our abilities, without getting permission from any public official to do so. Here we can follow the religion of our choice without interference or harassment by the government." And so on.

What I am trying to impress upon you is the fact that at the root of all our freedom, what we call our liberties, lie certain rights and guarantees that are set forth in the Constitution and embodied in our laws. Sometimes many of these are called civil rights. Their importance to us cannot possibly be overstated. There can be no true justice unless these principles are adhered to.

For example, when some particularly heinous or revolting crime has been committed or when we are faced with some public danger there is always pressure to cut corners by disregarding Constitutional guarantees or laws passed for the protection of all. Stand out against this, whether it be the doing or the omission to do something that deprives an accused of a fair trial, or an alleged illegal search and seizure, or the failure to admit a prisoner to proper bail, or deny him the right to counsel, or hold him an unreasonable time before preferring a specific charge against him. These seemingly procedural rules are part and parcel of what is, in truth and in fact, American freedom.

The privilege against self-incrimination extends to Communists as well as others who may be charged with crimes and their rights must be upheld no matter how mischievous or dangerous they may be. The historical reasons behind this part of our Bill of Rights are just as valid today as they were when that part of the Constitution was adopted. I would rather see every Communist go scot free than abandon or water down or in any manner diminish the force and vigor of a single one of our precious freedoms, and this particular one of which I speak is guaranteed by the Fifth Amendment.

The challenges to freedom today are different from those America faced in 1776. No tyrant imposes his will upon us from across the sea. But the struggle for freedom is neverending; in the very nature of human affairs the victory can never be completely won.

As a nation we are rich and powerful, but such is our passion for security and order that many of us would deal harshly, and if I may say so, unwisely, with those who seem to threaten our peace of mind, without pausing to consider that in the process we may lose or impair the vigor of those freedoms and liberties which are our surest weapons against the enemies beyond our borders and those within. We may forget that these freedoms and liberties are spiritual forces that are incredibly dynamic—

they are the motivation for action: action for the advancement of civilization, action to enhance the dignity and the usefulness of man and his capacity to live happily. Upon such spiritual forces as good will and freedom and justice our Republic was founded. They and not mere material wealth or physical force must guide our destiny in the years to come.

But someone of you may say: "these matters are no business of ours, let the judges see to it that justice is done." Yes, it is the business of the courts, I admit. The true sanctions, however, are in the hearts of the men and women who are America. You and I are part of America; we and all the millions of others like us, each and every single one, are duty-bound to live and think and act from day to day in such a way as to foster and cherish and nurture and preserve these freedoms. We must rededicate ourselves, without reservation of any kind, to the preservation of the rights of a free and independent people.

9 Argument Against Use of Television and Radio in Courtrooms

1954

I am not, in this matter, trying to tell legislators what to do or to get mixed up in a controversy of the sort judges should steer clear of. But every judge is interested in the administration of justice, and it is his sacred duty to keep the wells of justice pure and to do everything in his power to improve its processes and administration.

And so at the outset, I wish to make my point and then do the best I can to prove it.

What I say is this: Whenever there is a proceeding, the object of which is to ascertain the truth from conflicting testimony of witnesses and other proofs, whether it be in a courtroom or at a legislative hearing or anywhere else, the questioning of the witnesses before television apparatus, radio, and the like furnishes such an impediment and handicap that the ascertainment of the true facts becomes well-nigh impossible.

This delicate process of winnowing the wheat from the chaff, the true from the false, is complicated beyond belief because the law deals with humanity in the raw, and sometimes that is not a pretty sight.

There are other arguments against the use of television I would brush aside as in my judgment they merely confuse the central issue. It is said that the lights, the noise, and the heat and the batteries of apparatus are distracting and confusing. So they are.

But we have only to compare the technological conditions prevailing in the recent Army-McCarthy hearings with those of the Kefauver procedings a few years ago to appreciate the fact that advances in radio and television techniques will sooner or later eliminate objections based upon the presence of lights and cameras.

Then it is said that all concerned in the matter seize the opportunity for personal publicity and the airing of their pet views. But they do this to some extent in courtrooms, too.

And the converse is true. Witnesses object to the prying into their personal affairs, and claim they should have ample opportunity to state their own side in the matter in controversy, even where they are not parties or principals in the matter under investigation.

None of these complaints can fairly be leveled at television and radio. If there is injustice, it must be blamed on those conducting the trial or the hearing.

The real question is whether television and radio interfere with the ascertainment of the true facts.

With most of us the notion that a person should take the witness stand, swear to tell the truth, the whole truth, and nothing but the truth, and then make up a story out of whole cloth seems unbelievable, doesn't it? But they do and they do it every day in our courts throughout the land.

Our lives, our liberties, and our properties depend upon the exposure of these falsehoods. Some witnesses do this in a perfectly callous and cold-blooded way. They deliberately concoct their story, rehearse it, double check it, and then go ahead with it.

You have no idea how many crooks there are, some of them

highly intelligent and not seldom dressed in the height of fashion, I am sorry to say. Radio and television will never bother them. They are full of brass and they have the hide of a crocodile.

Most witnesses who give false testimony do it because they are so prejudiced they let their emotions take over and they really believe some of the things they say, or they embroider and add a few details here and there, omitting the parts that are troublesome. The whole gamut of humanity is involved in one way or another. The motives to conceal or fabricate are legion. And I know what I am talking about.

I am an expert in these matters. They are difficult, technical subjects, despite the fact that they look simple to those who know little about them.

I hope you begin to see how difficult it is to seek and find that sacred, precious thing—the truth. All the resources of the law, marshaled by a just, impartial, patient arbiter who presides over the contest with dignity and restraint, are none too ample for the task at hand, but when the judge and the witnesses and the lawyers or their counterparts in legislative hearings, for example, perform their functions before the microphones and batteries of floodlights knowing that perhaps ten millions of people or more are listening and watching their every move, the temptation to put on an act is almost irresistible. And that is what they do.

You have all seen it again and again in the recent proceedings which must still be fresh in the minds of everyone. Amidst all this confusion, with witnesses and interrogators making speeches, interrupting one another, tossing in asides, with or without looks of astonishment, surprise, dismay, or what not, how is one to find that submerged but precious kernel of truth?

The big fellow sees a bigger day ahead. The little fellow, whose testimony may be the most important of the lot, is in the limelight at last. The temptation to say something sensational is hard to put down. At least he may add a few minor conversations which never took place.

The timid, reticent witness whose testimony is difficult to elicit under the most favorable circumstances may shut up like a clam. But each and every one of them puts on an act.

Years ago the radio began to find its way into some of the courtrooms but that has now pretty generally been stopped. I well remember listening over the radio to the broadcast of the investigation by the Board of Steamboat Inspectors of the *Morro Castle* disaster. Remember the *Morro Castle*? Well, large numbers of witnesses were questioned. One of them, in the midst of his testimony, seized the microphone and said, "Mom—how am I doing?"

Well, that has all been stopped. Are we to go through the whole weary business of fighting it again now that the public has had a taste of what fun it is to watch proceedings over television?

Of course people like to see and hear these proceedings over radio and television. It is lots of fun and it is instructive too, in a way.

Because courtrooms are open to the public some people seem to think that the public has a right to have the proceedings televised and sent out over the radio, but there just isn't any such right. The reason our courts are open to the public is not to provide recreation or instruction in the ways of government but to prevent the possibility of Star Chamber proceedings where everything is secret and corruption or flagrant judicial abuses might flourish unseen and be impossible of detection and exposure.

It is just and right that the people should see the wheels of justice in motion and that the press should have free access to every court from the lowest to the highest. But the comings and goings of the members of the press are orderly and easily controlled. They present no such psychological barrier to the ascertainment of truth as do the radio and television.

98

When we started the trial of the eleven Communist leaders back in 1949, the courtroom was jammed. The fireworks started immediately. Someone made a motion to move the trial over to Madison Square Garden so all the workers could get in. They made quite an argument over this. It reminds me of the argument over television. They said the case was important, that everyone had a right to see it.

Well, let me add a word by way of conclusion. Our besetting sin is selfishness. Instead of applying the Golden Rule and fostering those spiritual forces such as good will and freedom and justice, which are, and since the founding of the Republic have been, our greatest strength, each of us keeps asking for things for himself, not caring very much about his neighbor. If a proceeding involving your own rights or your own personal liberty were to be conducted, would you not insist that every conceivable precaution be taken to make sure that the truth would prevail?

In presenting the case in opposition as it appeared to me I have tried to get at fundamentals—what we lawyers and judges call the jugular vein of the case. Does the use of radio and television in any substantial sense affect the process of ascertaining the truth when examining the witnesses or considering other proofs? I say it does, and that they constitute a psychological and very real barrier which for all practical purposes makes it impossible to get at the truth.

That is my point. That is my only point and be sure you get that. And because of this I would exclude them—not only from courtrooms, but from any other places where analogous efforts are being made to do justice on the basis of true facts.

That is where the legislative hearings come in. But the principle is the same, even if the place where the inquiry is pursued is the office of the manager of some business concern where a decision will be made on the subject of discharging an employee with people coming in and telling just what they saw and what they heard, or before the Baseball Commissioner who may be trying to find out who said what to an umpire. These come up, don't they? They have to be decided. The principles of justice and fair play are equally applicable to each of these situations.

10 The Spiritual Quality of Justice

1954

This concept of the spiritual quality of justice cuts pretty deep; but I wish to confess at the outset that I have none of the qualifications of a legal philosopher. My approach is simply that of a man who has caught hold of an idea and has quietly thought about it in the light of his own background and experience. As a matter of fact, I wish I were a philosopher. Again and again I have tried to embark on a steady course of reading on the subject of legal philosophy only to bog down in terminology and the endless sequences of names and quotations.

Basically, I shall be doing what I call preaching the gospel. The central thesis is very simple. I shall try to demonstrate the great importance of the ideal of justice in our society and its spiritual quality; and then do the best I can to explain what we as individuals can do about it. You may as well realize in the beginning that I think there is a great deal that we can do about it, and that our shortcomings are many and serious.

One of the men who has influenced me over the years is my former colleague on the Law Faculty at Columbia University, Professor Elliott Cheatham. He is one of those rare souls who

101

has within himself a love of justice so intense that it affects everyone with whom he comes in contact.

Well, Professor Cheatham has noted that those societies which have endured in world history, and have managed to survive crises such as that facing democracy today, have been those which were founded upon and motivated by great ideals. In our society, for example, one of the most fundamental of these ideals is a composite which I have referred to as the "Spiritual Quality of Justice." But great ideals alone, Professor Cheatham points out, are not enough. These ideals must be expressed, must become woven into the social fabric. Such expression is achieved partly in the law, which gives these ideals coherence. Thus, for example, all the philosophizing in the world about personal liberty is in actual practice not worth a farthing without the concrete embodiment of the results of such philosophizing in our Bill of Rights.

However, a still further—and, as far as we lawyers are concerned, a most important—step remains. For it is not enough for society to have ideals, even when these ideals are translated into a series of binding laws. It is necessary in addition that these laws then be applied to the myriad situations of human life. This in large part is the function of the lawyer.

In the realm of human affairs there are no absolutes, nothing is static. All is change, development, growth, and decay. What I would impress upon you first is the fact that ideals and laws and the functioning of laws by definition and necessity exist, not in a vacuum or in some theoretical utopia, but only in the minds and in the deeds of individual men and women. In such matters each of us has a nondelegable and a very real responsibility.

A word of warning before we proceed. I shall be skipping here and there, running around Robin Hood's barn as it were, and you will probably think I am aimlessly ad-libbing and that I have forgotten what I started to say. Don't worry about this; it is just my way of approaching a subject on the bias. The direct approach is never quite as effective, whether you are bringing up children or arguing to a jury or trying to formulate a theme such as this.

The Ideal of Justice as a Dynamic Force in Society

At one time or another probably every single member of the community has meditated upon the subject of the difference between law and justice. Hidden behind the quips and jokes about lawyers and judges and the administration of justice generally there is a deep-seated feeling, ranging anywhere from mere suspicion to deep conviction, that somehow or other the vast mills of the law grind out judgments and statutes and practices and procedures which essentially fail to achieve justice. I venture to say that there are few sufferings more poignant than those of the man who knows in his soul that he is in the right but who comes out of an altercation with society or with his neighbors or from a lawsuit with a decision against him.

It is bad enough when one of us feels that he has been unjustly dealt with by his friends or his business associates and his adversaries in the ebb and flow of life. But the experience is devastating when the injustice, whether real or fancied, has been or seems to have been perpetrated by the very system supposedly designed by organized society for our protection.

Some of this is due, of course, to the fallibility of the human animal. It is possible for a person to think he is right when in fact he is wrong; it is possible for juries and for judges to make mistakes. And no amount of tinkering with the rules of the game and the formulation of the laws and improving the procedures for the administration of justice will ever wholly eliminate the possibility of error.

What I wish to emphasize here at the outset is the downright suffering of the person unjustly dealt with by society. Here, I believe, is the origin and the source of all the speculation on the subject of law and justice. And I am talking about what goes on in the mind of the ordinary person, whether he is a businessman or a mechanic or a college professor or a manicurist.

The curious part of all this is that the very people who thus speculate on the subject and who are convinced that the law is one thing and justice something different, fail to realize that the people of every race and every geographical section of the world have devised their particular system of laws and all the complicated procedures which go hand in hand with the administration of justice everywhere for the special purpose of achieving justice. We must put that down for a fact.

There is no such thing as achieving justice by the process of merely trying to be fair in particular situations.

I remember when I was a boy in school reading Caesar's *Commentaries*. When the troops went into their winter quarters Caesar went back to one of the larger communities in Gaul and held the assizes. I used to wonder what he did there and what the assizes were. Well, it is all very simple. He held court and this meant that he sat on a sort of an elevated throne and the people came before him and he heard each side and then handed down his decision out of hand. Doubtless he tried to do the right thing, but it does not require much imagination to realize that he must often have been influenced by the exigencies of his military plans and position and his executive power as the Roman deputy. And it is a curious fact that in world history we so often find the executive and the judicial power residing in the same persons, despite the manifest inconsistency.

And so if we place ourselves in the position of those who tried to struggle with this problem in primitive societies we can see how laws and systems of laws gradually emerged. And one does not have to be very learned or very profound to realize that inevitably the judges and lawyers or priests, or whoever they were, spent a good deal of their time formulating rules of procedure. To avoid confusion and chaos there had to be ways of doing things in administering laws. To the insiders who were the only ones who understood such matters these masses of procedural technicalities have always been a happy hunting ground. Of course, the initiates never denied that the merits of the case and the application of the governing rule of substantive law were matters of first importance. But the merits had a way of getting lost in the fog. There were rules about how to get the case before a judge, rules about the formulation of the claim and the defense, rules about who should go first and who should go last, rules about the deliberations of jurors, and so on. Just imagine having a rule that the jury must go without food or light or goodness knows what else while deliberating upon their verdict.

The undoubted fact is that lawyers and judges like to play with these things, and when they have once mastered the intricacies of any particular system of procedure it is only human nature for them to perpetuate their monopoly, if they can.

In the old days, and the time of which I speak is within my own lifetime, all the law students in all the law schools had to study common law pleading. What a system for the doing of injustice! And yet Coke and Littleton and all the lawyers and judges of their time reveled in these niceties and thought the system must have been of divine origin. But the people who were thrown out of court on one technicality after another must have suffered the tortures of the damned.

No system of laws designed by man has ever been perfect. The quest for justice is like the search for truth; it goes on and on endlessly. There is always work to be done in the vineyard. And I verily believe that of all the instances where justice has fallen short of its mark, perhaps a majority have been due to defects and shortcomings in matters of procedure.

When I used to try jury cases I found a very effective approach was to remind the jurors that, as a matter of fact, most members of the community go through their whole lives, from beginning to end, in a more or less humdrum fashion. They live with their families and they go to business every day and they have a certain amount of fun and recreation; but really nothing of an unusual or dramatic character ever happens to them. But every once in a while something does happen, perhaps an automobile accident or a murder or a fire, and then the particular persons involved become the actors in one of these exciting dramas of real life which wind up in the courtroom.

In just this eccentric, haphazard fashion something suddenly happens to some of us which touches off the spark and arouses within us that burning zeal for justice, which should be in the bosom of everyone, and especially lawyers and judges. When thus the lightning strikes, a spiritual force is generated and the result is apt to be that the person having this experience dedicates himself from that moment onwards to the doing of justice.

The idea that I wish to put across is that justice truly is a spiritual force, that it is dynamic. It is this dynamic force that gets people to do things. When it once possesses us, the conscious perpetration of injustice becomes impossible. When motivated by this burning zeal for justice of which I speak, the mere winning of a lawsuit, the mere victory over one's opponent becomes quite secondary to the doing of what is essentially righteous and just.

The way spiritual forces function is really wonderful. For a long time they lie dormant as though nonexistent. But when brought to life, they work with devastating effect. The plain ordinary man of today becomes the crusader of tomorrow and miracles are in the making.

But for the experience I went through when thousands and thousands of letters poured in upon me after the trial of the

107

Communist leaders in 1949, I would never have thought of the spiritual quality of justice. One must feel the impact of the power of a spiritual force to realize its potential.

Here and there over the length and breadth of these United States are individuals in considerable numbers who have been bitten by this bug. Sometimes it is the result of participating in the work of the Legal Aid Society. Sometimes a lawyer acts as assigned counsel to defend someone charged with crime and the effort made, without other reward than the satisfaction of fighting for justice, does the trick. Some lawyers will not touch a negligence case or a divorce case or one steeped in sordid, unpleasant circumstances. But doctors are not supposed thus to pick and choose. Nor should we lawyers do so. In the midst of the seamy side of life many a lawyer has come to feel stir within him this spiritual force.

The lightning first struck me in the first case I ever tried. It was a little case in the Municipal Court in Brooklyn, for the recovery of five hundred dollars which I alleged had been procured from my client by fraud. The facts were very simple. My client, a young man of about twenty-seven, had seen an advertisement in one of the New York papers to the effect that anyone having five hundred dollars to invest would get some very interesting information at such and such a place. Having just five hundred dollars in a savings bank he answered the advertisement and was shown some acetylene gas articles such as lamps, irons, and so on, and was told that he could have the exclusive agency of the State of New Jersey in the selling of these articles on behalf of the sole manufacturer. The five hundred dollars was supposed to be put up as security for his integrity. He made the contract, put up the five hundred dollars, and was given a little box containing samples of the articles he was to sell. When he went to New Jersey and tried to sell these articles he found that they were on sale in various stores at retail at prices lower than he was paying, which, of course, made it impossible for him to make any profit, or indeed to make any sales at all except at a loss. The person or corporation which had his money was not the sole manufacturer. On the basis of these false representations I sued to recover the five hundred dollars. We had a jury of six and everything went swimmingly in my presentation of the plaintiff's case. I even had a schoolteacher from Pennsylvania who had been defrauded in the same way, by the same defendant, and she made quite an impression on the jury. I noticed that my adversary did not seem to be putting up much of a fight. In any event, I rested at the close of the plaintiff's case, and my adversary then said merely, "I move to dismiss the complaint." There was no statement of any reasons, there was no discussion, and the judge said, "Motion granted."

I was bewildered and dismayed. Before I could even collect my thoughts and my papers on the counsel table the trial of the next case started.

I had no premonition of the tragedy that was to come, but, as the result of that ruling, my client went out and shot himself. I was so frightened that I did not even tell my wife about it, or anyone else for a space of some fifteen years. I am not sure that I did not destroy the papers, for I have never been able to find them.

A little reflection and further study showed me the problem in all its simplicity. My suit must of necessity have been based upon an affirmance or disaffirmance of the contract. If based upon a disaffirmance there should have been a tender of the box containing perhaps twenty-five dollars worth of samples. I had made no tender. On the basis of affirmance it was incumbent upon me to prove my damages by offering testimony of the value of the contents of the box. I had not done that either. I was inclined to take all the blame for the tragedy upon myself.

But as I look back and as I realize how easy it would have been to supply the necessary proof had my adversary specified the grounds of his motion or had the judge indicated the

109

reasons for his ruling, I am inclined to think today that there is something wrong with the system of laws which makes it possible for such things to happen. And in my small way I have been trying to do something about the subject ever since.

When I was in law school the case system was just beginning to be generally accepted and put in operation. Langdell and Ames and those other giants in the Harvard Law School had revolutionized legal education. The general ferment had begun to operate. But we were still in the good old days when the great body of the law was supposed to be a system approaching perfection, with all its parts functioning in perfect harmony, with logic and reason in full sway.

We boys (for no women were allowed in the law schools in those days) were fascinated by the body of rules in the particular subjects of substantive law and we learned them with every assurance that they would be permanent and indestructible. Of course we heard something of improvements and changes in the laws to meet new conditions, but not too much. In those days it was my ambition to be a great conveyancer and I remember studying about contingent remainders, executory devises, and springing uses; and I even read through the full report of the long debate of the judges of England on the rule in Shelley's case and Fearne's massive work on Contingent Remainders. The only fire that burned in our breasts as far as I can recall, was the zeal to become good craftsmen and technicians of the law, to master the decisions and the statutes and the various rules of law and procedure so that we might go downtown and get good jobs in the leading law offices and, in the course of time, win cases from the other lawyers who were our contemporaries and our elders. I never heard a word that I can recall from the time I entered law school until I left, about the spiritual quality of justice and the importance of working for the ends of justice. Not that we were taught to be unscrupulous or unethical; quite the contrary. And individual members of the faculty gave us some inkling about what justice really meant. But there was no studied, persistent, formal effort to train us for the dedication of ourselves to justice.

And I say, with all the emphasis at my command, that the law schools of today are still in the same old rut. It is when we are young and impressionable that our characters and our ideals are formed. No amount of reading and studying the Canons of Ethics will arouse in the breasts of law students the spiritual fire of which I speak. There must be some systematic reconsideration of this problem in terms of law school curricula and the teaching of the individual courses. It is not enough that here and there an individual teacher devotes himself to this task and makes his own life an example for the enlightenment of others. The subject is too important for casual and haphazard, hit-and-miss treatment.

We must not forget this spiritual quality of justice, this dedication of ourselves to justice lies at the roots of our beloved American democracy. It is embedded in our Constitution as well as in the Declaration of Independence. Our survival as a nation may well depend upon the development of our spiritual resources, in keeping with our heritage from the founders.

Procedural Reform and the Achievement of Justice

When my colleague, United States Circuit Judge Charles E. Clark, sometimes referred to as the father of the Federal Rules of Civil Procedure, heard that I was writing on this matter he remarked that he hoped I would deal with some of the "earthy" subjects. And that is what I had intended all along to do. The connection between spiritual things and earthy things is not always by way of contrast. For example, it would be a marvelous thing if those of us who profess to be Christians would really follow the teachings of Christ in our daily comings and goings, in the little earthy things we do all day, every day. But we need help and guidance and leadership, if good will, tolerance, and the Golden Rule are to be behind our every thought and deed.

We have already observed that no amount of theorizing and no amount of care in the formulation of rules of law will suffice to eliminate miscarriages of justice due to the fallibility of man. No less an authority than Chief Justice Arthur T. Vanderbilt supports my assertion that the dissatisfaction on the part of the public with established principles of substantive law is as nothing compared with the dissatisfaction with the multitude of procedural inadequacies which bedevil the judicial process. We may as well frankly face the fact that these technicalities stem from the same old trouble, the fallibility of man. It is just plain human nature which leads us to turn away from the difficult, troublesome task, if we can. It is much easier to resort to some rule of procedure to dispose of a case, rather than to dig into the merits, which more often than not involve intricate problems of credibility.

Some of the more important of these procedural inadequacies, especially those which are hardly ever given formal treatment in the traditional curriculum of the typical American law school, are indeed earthy subjects, as you shall see. They are tough, thorny, and difficult of solution. Their importance will be self-evident.

First in importance is the selection of judges and the making of provisions for their tenure, compensation, and retirement. A corollary subject is the selection of jurors, providing them with suitable quarters and accommodations, and the formulation of methods designed to obtain general jury panels which represent a true cross section of the community. Next, the business management of the courts, by court integration, Judicial Councils, and by the establishment of an administrative office or director or executive assistant to the Chief Justice. Fourth, judicial regulation of procedure by giving the rule-making power to the highest court of a state and taking it away from the legislature.

Incidental questions, to which we shall not have time to give more than passing reference, but which are part of the general pattern, relate to the preliminary training and the licensing of attorneys and counselors-at-law, bar integration, the general simplification of procedure, and the development of new devices such as pretrial conferences and summary judgments.

It is universally recognized that our particular brand of democracy cannot function without judges and courts to interpret our constitutions and our laws and to maintain the equality of all before the bar of justice. And it should follow, as the night the day, that we should select as judges of the entire judicial hierachy, from the lowest to the highest, only those who have the best qualification to be judges, and that the selection should be made on the basis of merit alone. But the fact is otherwise. And bear in mind that I recognize that we have large numbers of judges of the highest type. I am not attacking the judges; but I do say the existing system leaves much to be desired.

The background is interesting. The founders realized the

importance of an independent judiciary. One of the complaints against George III in the Declaration of Independence was that:

> He has made the judges dependent upon his will alone for the tenure of their offices and the amount and payment of their salaries.

And so it was that the Constitutional provisions of ten of the original thirteen states and of eight of the eleven new ones admitted before 1830 gave life tenure or tenure "during good behavior" to their judges.

But the effect of the Jacksonian Revolution, from 1830 to 1850, was disastrous. Here is a comment by James Bryce, writing in 1899:

> Any one of the phenomena I have described—popular elections, short term, and small salaries—would be sufficient to lower the character of the judiciary. Popular elections throw the choice into the hands of political parties, that is to say, of knots of wire-pullers inclined to use every office as a means of rewarding political services, and garrisoning with grateful partisans posts which may conceivably become of political importance. Short terms oblige the judge to remember and keep on good terms with those who made him what he is, and in whose hands his fortunes lie. They induce timidity, they discourage independence.

It would be a weary and unprofitable task to recount the seemingly endless steps taken here and there to reduce the common law powers of the judges; and this must inevitably have resulted in some diminution in their general stature and dignity. The adoption in New York of the Code of Civil Procedure, harnessing the judges with over 3,000 Sections containing the most detailed provisions governing every step and reducing flexibility to a minimum, was part of the process; and

114

this set off a chain reaction of codes in a large number of other states, especially the new ones.

Whatever may have been the course of development of this historical sequence, the undoubted fact today is that there is now a tie-up between the judiciary and partisan politics which I believe to be fundamentally wrong. I am not particularly interested in whether the judges are appointed by the state executive or elected by the people. In New York, where the governor appoints to preelection vacancies, the results over the years have been about the same. With some exceptions he generally takes the man selected by the local political leaders. What I am interested in is getting the judges out of partisan politics, lock, stock, and barrel.

Of course the politicians are against this. I don't blame them, nor do I accuse them of any wrongdoing. All jobs are grist for the political mill and judgeships are the juiciest of the lot. Moreover, the whole political apparatus, including most of the judges themselves, especially those in the lower civil and criminal courts, are in favor of maintaining the status quo. But plain Mr. and Mrs. John Doe and all the other ordinary citizens who have no axes to grind and who instinctively look upon their judges with affection and even with reverence are and always will be opposed to any avoidable connection between the judiciary and partisan politics.

The reasons are not far to seek. Everyone knows that in vast areas of the country, and especially so in New York, the political leaders and not the electorate select the judges. Whether or not there is justification for it—and I readily admit that almost always there is none—the average man thinks some of the judges are subject to influence. It is not enough that the judges in fact be men of integrity; it is of equal importance that they be thought to be so. Chief Justice Vanderbilt often refers to a Gallup Poll which indicated that twenty-eight percent of those answering the inquiry stated that they did not

115

believe their local criminal judges were honest. As a matter of fact, the fixing of traffic tickets has approached the point of being a national scandal.

Think of the benefits which must accrue to the judges themselves were such a separation of the judiciary from partisan politics to become an accomplished fact. The increase in independence and dignity is too plain for argument. Leaders of the bar, many of whom come from humble beginnings, would more readily accept judicial positions when freed from any sense of obligation. The removal of the burden of participation in party politics would leave the judges more time for the uninterrupted performance of judicial duties for which they were chosen and for which they are paid their salaries.

As a matter of fact, plans for removing the judges as far as possible from partisan politics are under consideration in a large number of states at this very time. There is a California system already in operation. The Missouri plan is probably the most successful. Other proposals are being studied in Indiana, Kentucky, Michigan, Minnesota, New Jersey, New Mexico, North Carolina, Pennsylvania, South Carolina, West Virginia, and Wisconsin; and there is discussion of the subject by Bar groups in nearly every state of the Union.

It is interesting to know that all this stemmed from a resolution by the House of Delegates of the American Bar Association in 1937, recommending that vacancies be filled preliminarily by appointment by the state executive "from a list named by another agency, composed in part of high judicial officers and in part of other citizens, selected for the purpose, who hold no other office." The appointees, under this plan, after a relatively brief period in which the voters have an opportunity to evaluate their abilities on the basis of actual performance, are submitted to the approval of the electorate without the endorsement of any political party. It is typical of most of the plans now under discussion that the judges be elected without party labels, that they be not permitted to

116

hold office in any political party during their judicial tenure, and that they be forbidden to contribute money or services, directly or indirectly, to any political party or organization, or to take part in any political campaign.

This sounds like the millennium, doesn't it? Well, it may well come to pass if enough people get bitten by the bug I was talking about.

I could go on about paying the judges decent salaries, increasing their tenure of office where the terms of office are now too short, and making suitable provision for retirement. I have seen instances of judges in their late seventies and eighties who hold on only because they would have nothing to live on if they resigned, but I must content myself with the mere mention of these subjects as part of the composite picture.

As for the jury system, it is one of our fundamental institutions; and most of us take it for granted and go about our business. It is well to remember that trial by jury is gradually going out of vogue in England where almost all civil cases are now tried by judges alone; and there are many here in the United States who think juries are easily bamboozled and that jury trials involve a lot of waste time and effort.

I happen to be one of those who believe in the jury system; I believe in our people and I trust them. From my point of view laws permitting majority verdicts—as in New York where in civil cases a vote of ten jurors is sufficient for a verdict—represent a disintegration of the jury system. I would insist upon a unanimous verdict in all cases, civil and criminal; and I would abolish Blue Ribbon juries wherever permitted by state law. Fortunately we do not have especially selected panels in the federal system. Moreover, service as a juror helps to train men and women as citizens of a free country and is one of the things that make American democracy work.

But all this depends upon getting the right type of juror and giving jurors, during their period of service and during their deliberations, proper accommodations and proper protection.

It is surprising how little attention has been paid to these important matters by legal scholars.

The fundamentals are simple enough. Jurors should be honest and possessed of sufficient intelligence to understand the issues as submitted to them by the judge, and they must be selected in a manner reasonably calculated to produce in the general jury panel a fair cross section of the community.

Perhaps it was inevitable that the methods of selecting jurors should vary as much as they do. After all, there are essential differences between urban and rural communities, and local conditions even in adjoining counties often justify quite different methods of approach.

But there must be some systematic weeding-out process by the commissioner of jurors or whoever it is who does the selecting. A good definition of a fit juror is one who is "physically and mentally healthy, possessing a good reputation for honesty and morality with at least enough education to be able to read, write, and understand English; and finally of sufficient intelligence and experience in life to be able to understand the various problems presented in both civil and criminal litigation."

I was told, when in Louisville a few years ago, that it was not uncommon to have the official go out on the street and corral a few jurors every once in a while.

During the depression years it was mighty difficult, at least in New York, to get a jury not composed of twelve unemployed persons.

The suspicion is sometimes expressed that some prosecutors have stricken from the jury rolls all persons who have voted for a verdict of acquittal.

There is always some likelihood that workers for a daily wage may not be able to afford to serve as jurors where the jury fees are too small, and that businessmen and others who would ordinarily make excellent jurors beg off with one excuse or another.

118

When I presided over the trial of the eleven Communist leaders we had a panel of some three hundred odd jurors to pick from. The first thing I did was to ask those who did not wish to serve to give their excuses. The result was that every single businessman or woman or person with a position of responsibility asked to be excused. I was positively ashamed. True, it was likely to be a long trial, but in a democracy such as ours we must all make some sacrifices.

One of the soft spots is the almost incredible number of exemptions from jury duty provided by the laws of the various states. There is no uniformity about these exemptions, but viewed in the large they include: lawyers and their clerks, stenographers, and secretaries; physicians; dentists; pharmacists or druggists; embalmers, undertakers, morticians, or funeral directors; optometrists; chiropractors and osteopaths; veterinarians; nurses; teachers and professors; clergymen; certified public accountants; actuaries; newspaper reporters, editors, publishers, printers, and linotype operators; radio announcers and engineers; certain railroad employees; seamen, pilots, and steamboat personnel; ferryboat men; employees of telephone or telegraph companies; express company workers; bank tellers, cashiers, and bank presidents; millers; government officials; firemen; national guardsmen and militiamen; police; attendants in institutions such as almshouses, state hospitals and asylums; mail carriers and postal employees; jail employees; fish and game wardens; forestry agents; customs house officers; coroners; and overseers of roads.

This doesn't make sense, does it? Everyone with a legitimate reason may be excused in any event. These exemptions should be cut down radically if we are to get the best possible jurors. And we need the best qualified jurors just as we need the best qualified judges.

Then there is the matter of the business management of the courts. The administration of justice in the United States is big business. The number of judges, commissioners, bailiffs,

119

attendants, secretaries, criers, and miscellaneous assistants runs into the thousands in the federal and state judicial establishments. There are all sorts of disbursements for salaries, maintenance of buildings, traveling expenses, books and supplies, and the keeping of records.

Every successful business has a business manager who knows the conditions of his business and then plans for the future. He knows his inventory at any given time, he knows the amount of income and outgo, he knows the speed of operation. Also he knows his personnel and the work load in each department. He has meetings of his officers and department heads to consult about the condition of the business as a whole. It seems elementary that there should be similar good business management of our judicial establishments. But by and large there is not. This is one of the most pressing of all the present-day problems of judicial administration.

The source of the difficulty is pretty plain. In many of the states with large population and with their roots in the colonial period, such as New York, Massachusetts, Pennsylvania, and Virginia, the judicial system is composed of a vast number of courts with various jurisdictions, each jealous of its own independence and anxious to keep external control down to a minimum. The judges of these various courts differ widely in ability, industry, and experience. In some localities the dockets are traditionally congested, sometimes as much as four or five years in arrears; in other sections there is little judicial business and pressure of work much less exacting. Control over the financing of these various courts rests in a great variety of public bodies, and political considerations have great weight in the making of many of the appointments of court personnel. There is no way of estimating the amount of waste but it must necessarily run into large figures. No commercial business could be successfully conducted in such a haphazard way and without some executive and administrative control.

The ideal way to deal with this situation is the combination of a single integrated state court, such as exists in New Jersey, supplemented by an administrative office or director, acting under the orders of the chief justice. With such a set-up the number of courts is reduced, each has charge of a given segment of the judicial case load, and shifts can readily be made whenever there is more or less work to be done in any one of the various divisions or departments or where certain judges have exceptional skill and experience in a certain type of work. The effect in New Jersey has been almost unbelievable. With twenty percent fewer judges after the new constitution of 1948 took effect, ninety percent more cases were disposed of in the first year of operations and an additional twenty percent in the second year. Practically all the dockets were brought up-to-date and delays in disposition of cases disappeared.

Naturally, this was not accomplished without a good deal of weeping and wailing and gnashing of teeth. Lawyers by constitutional habit are disposed to put cases off again and again, and the judges like to see a little light ahead. But there was general rejoicing by the public at large.

The way improvements are generally made is by the tinkering process. Whenever conditions get so bad as to approach the point of a public scandal, action is taken reshuffling the cards to some extent, permitting a limited assignment of judges to some court other than their own or increasing or limiting the jurisdiction of one or more of the courts having some special jurisdiction. But the real answer is a single integrated state court with a chief justice at the top with power to act.

In the federal system the Administrative Office of the United States Courts, created in 1939 by the Administrative Office Act, has done a magnificent job. It is charged with the duty of setting up and presenting the budget of the courts to Congress after approval by the Judicial Conference of the

United States; of auditing the accounts of clerks of courts, United States commissioners, the referees in bankruptcy, and other officials in the court system; of furnishing the judges with supplies, law books, and equipment; the accumulation of statistical data and the making of reports on calendar conditions and the arrears of the particular judges; and it acts as a sort of secretariat or agent for the Judicial Conference. As a matter of fact, the influence of the Administrative Office goes beyond the business routine and is exerted toward sound standards of performance by all those coming under its supervision.

By setting up the Judicial Conference of the United States, presided over by the chief justice and composed of the chief judges of the Courts of Appeals of the eleven circuits, supplemented by the Judicial Councils, and the Judicial Conferences of the Circuits, which I shall not pause to describe, there is provided opportunity for discussion of the miscellaneous problems of the courts and for the making of suggestions for improvements in the administration of justice in the United States courts.

The success of the Administrative Office has been so widely recognized that movements have been started in many of the states in recent years to adapt it to local state conditions. A state may take as little or as much of this federal prototype as it may desire or as it may be in a position to finance; and this flexibility has been one of the most attractive features. The terminology often reflects a certain amount of local pride, and we seldom see the man in charge called the "director." More often he is the "assistant to the chief justice" or the "executive secretary" or something of the sort.

Finally, under the heading of business management of the courts, we come to judicial councils. They are not at all like the Judicial Councils under the Administrative Office Act which I mentioned a moment ago. Those consist of the circuit judges in each of the eleven federal circuits and they supervise the work of the United States District Courts in their circuit. Judicial councils generally are bodies created by state law to gather statistics, discuss current problems, and formulate studies and specific proposed legislation or proposed state constitutional amendments to implement suggested reforms in judicial administration. The membership of these judicial councils has often been composed of the head judicial officers of the highest and intermediate appellate courts, some members of the legislature, some leading lawyers, and a few prominent and civic-minded laymen. Their influence has generally been good but not spectacular. Occasionally, as in New York, the judicial council, for one reason or another which has not been clear to me, gets at odds with the legislature and few of its recommendations are adopted.

This matter of business management of the courts is really one of paramount importance, but it is difficult to make it interesting and to get people excited about it. Lawyers and Bar groups generally bog down in matters of detail, and so many ways of doing the job are suggested that nothing whatever is accomplished. The secret of success, I think, is in leadership and coöperation with the lay public. That is how Chief Justice Vanderbilt beat the opposition in New Jersey.

Judicial regulation of procedure is another tough one and it really should not be tough at all. Lawyers and judges who come here from other countries are simply amazed to find one system of procedure in the federal courts and about twenty-five other systems of procedure flourishing merrily in the various state courts. Of course, it was worse under the old Conformity Act, when you never could tell how much of the local procedure was in force in the local federal courts.

What a boon it would be to have a single uniform system of civil and criminal procedure applicable throughout the entire United States! Someday we shall see it. Nothing is impossible. We finally got rid of prohibition.

The way to do it is to have each law school conduct a basic

course on civil procedure founded upon the Federal Rules of Civil Procedure. The local practice should be subsidiary and incidental. After all, it is hard to imagine a successful lawyer without some cases in the federal courts. The Federal Rules must sooner or later be mastered, and in my judgment they represent the very best we have. Grounded in these rules the boys and girls who go out from the law schools every year will sooner or later have positions of sufficient influence to do the trick.

There never was any sense in the promulgation of an infinite variety of procedural details by the legislature. Competence and disinterestedness in such matters are in the judges; and the judges of the highest court of a state, aided by an advisory committee of lawyers, who consult with and receive suggestions from the Bar generally, are the people to whom this important task should be delegated. As long as the legislature has control of matters of procedure there will continue to be the usual pulling and hauling, lobbying, and so on, with a few jokers popping out every now and then which look innocent enough on their face but which always turn out to benefit some special interest.

I have lived to see effort after effort to obtain a short and flexible practice act and rules defeated in New York. The judges do not want the Federal Rules, the lawyers do not want the Federal Rules. But the day will come when the people will stand up on their hind legs and follow some crusader who wishes to be done with these masses of technicalities, and they will go. That is where the spiritual part comes in. When the fire within burns brightly, the impossible becomes easy.

It is high time that the students and the professors in the law schools became aware of these pressing problems of judicial administration. What I have been describing in this very sketchy way is part of the Program of the Section of Judicial Administration of the American Bar Association, of which I was chairman a few years ago. Just let those interested get to-

124

gether with that crowd some day if they wish to see a group of men dedicated to the cause of justice. Judges like Arthur Vanderbilt of New Jersey, John Parker of North Carolina, Ira Jayne of Michigan, Bolitha Laws of the District of Columbia, Charles Clark of Connecticut, James Douglas and Laurence Hyde of Missouri, and Edward Hudgins, Chief Justice of the Supreme Court of Appeals of Virginia; law professors and law school deans like Seasongood of Cincinnati, Pirsig of Minnesota, Cheatham of Columbia, Sunderland of Michigan, Storey of Texas, Harno of Illinois, and a host of others; to say nothing of lawyers like Harry Nims of New York, and others from almost every state of the Union.

The law students and professors should know more about the minimum standards of judicial administration for which the Section of Judicial Administration has been fighting so manfully. Just let them look up some of these names in the law library and read some of their books and their law review articles. These men are fearless, they are independent, they are disinterested—and they believe in America, as do I.

Contributions by Individuals to Justice—The Law Student, The Lawyer, The Judge, The Citizen

We now approach the third and last step in Professor Cheatham's formula for survival. We must have ideals; they must become imbedded in laws binding upon society, and they must be brought to realization or fruition through individual actions. If you or I are bitten by the bug and have within our souls this burning zeal for justice, what can we do about it? Take the law student, for example.

When a young man enters law school he is at once on sacred, hallowed ground. From that day on he is an integral part of the administration of justice. Just as the medical student must go through many an unsavory experience, so does the law student come in contact with all the evil, all the connivance and wrongdoing that the ingenuity of man has been able to conceive. There will be opened up before him an unending vista of ways to cheat and defraud and ways to defeat justice by resorting to tricky tactics or taking advantage of the inexperienced and the unwary. These things we must learn if we are to serve our clients well and preserve their rights. But woe to him who thinks the resort to such devices will bring him success at the Bar! Nothing is more precious to a lawyer than a reputation for integrity and as a true lover of justice. Once besmirched, the stain is almost never quite eradicated.

The right attitude of mind from the very beginning is half the battle won. With every case and every principle of law in every course, the law student must ask himself the question whether the result is just, whether it could have been avoided, whether it is good for society.

It is very important that in his every thought and act, toward his fellow students, law professors, and everyone with whom he comes in contact, he try his level best to be fair and just.

If some opportunity appears to participate in Legal Aid work, on however humble a basis, he must not let it pass. One must have close contact with the trials and problems and sufferings of others if one is to respond sympathetically, as a lawyer should. The more experience one can get performing services without any fee the better.

Then there is the matter of grades. What shall I say about them? Sometimes I wish they could be abolished so that teacher and student alike could study solely for the purpose of finding the truth and giving expression to it. Surely the student who works for grades alone makes a grievous mistake, as he is apt to be interested only in knowing what the professor wants him to say or rather what he thinks the professor wants him to say.

When my jury work finally made further law teaching impossible, I came, in 1940 after twenty-five years of active service, to my last lecture at Columbia Law School. One of the subjects I discussed was grades, and I said, "Brains are cheap," and so they truly are. You can always hire someone to do a good technical job. The real rewards are reserved for those with loyalty, courage, and plenty of "guts."

If a student keeps thinking of the spiritual quality of justice perhaps some day the bug will bite him too. When that once happens he never recovers.

And I can assure you that the life of a lawyer is a most exciting and a most rewarding experience.

The congestion of court dockets and the general gumming up of the whole machinery of justice is due in no small measure to the fact that thousands upon thousands of lawsuits are brought by people who know they have no just claim but who hope to frighten or to badger those whom they sue into making some settlement, which in many cases is no more than paying tribute to blackmail. Probably something of the kind was going on in the days of the Pharaohs. But the practice has reached formidable proportions in these complicated modern

127

times. The cumulative effect of this sort of thing on the administration of justice is serious. The disintegration of the moral fiber of the person who brings such a lawsuit is bad enough. But the man who is sued is faced with the expense of hiring a lawyer and it is the dread that the processes of the law may afford him no protection that leads to the payment of what is euphemistically called "nuisance value," and sometimes more, depending upon what harassing tactics may do to impress the victim with the uncertainty of jury verdicts and other pitfalls of the law. This in turn leads to cynicism and a general feeling that the forces of evil will prevail in any event and that one may as well bow before the storm.

It is my personal belief that these holdups have their origin chiefly in a disintegration of public morals, but the blame is laid at the doors of the lawyers. And there is some justification for this, as the services of a lawyer are generally needed before any case can be brought to court.

And so I say to the lawyers as item one in my list of what each can personally contribute to the achievement of justice: never participate in any manner, shape, or form in one of these unrighteous proceedings, which are based not on any merit, but on the hope that the person sued will pay something to avoid the trouble and expense of defending the action or because he fears that he may lose because of some precedural inadequacy. These strike suits stab justice in the back and they help to spread the false doctrine that there is no justice.

Please do not misunderstand me. I do not mean that no claim should be brought to court unless the claimant is sure of success. Whenever there is a fair and reasonable controversy on the law or the facts it is the proper business of the courts to decide it. That is what courts are for. Probably, too, there is as much (if not more) bearing of false witness by defendants as by plaintiffs. What I do mean is that there is something sacred about justice, something truly spiritual, and

128

every lawyer must be constantly alert to see that what he does supports justice rather than defeats it.

Professor Cheatham says that it is not enough that we have ideals, they must be applied to the countless situations which confront human beings in their daily life. Think of what the good lawyers can do if they proceed with their professional duties in the spirit of complete and utter dedication to justice! This applies to the drafting of agreements, the adjustment of differences, the preparation of wills, and the settlement of estates, as well as to the trial of lawsuits in court.

Another thing lawyers can do is to serve the courts as assigned counsel in defending without compensation those who are charged with crime but who are without means to employ a lawyer. This is especially important where the cause is unpopular and the defendant is charged with some odious or revolting crime.

In New Jersey they are trying out a plan by which all members of the Bar are assigned to defend these cases in rotation, some acting as trial counsel and some as assistants. It is hard to picture a real estate lawyer or a skilled draftsman of complicated wills defending a pickpocket, but they say the system is working out in a satisfactory way.

I had one of those experiences during World War II when I was assigned by Chief Judge C. Knox of the United States District Court for the Southern District of New York (where I later served as a judge) to defend a man charged with treason for having had some dealings with the men who came in submarines from Germany to destroy our aluminum industry. The man's name was Anthony Cramer.

For a long time I felt pretty sorry for myself. There was a lot about the case in the newspapers and I noticed that some of my friends began to avoid me. There were some very audible comments to the general effect that perhaps I was a traitor too; of course Harold Medina wasn't doing all this for nothing, and so on. But as I delved into the complicated subject of treason and became convinced of the man's innocence, there came a feeling of satisfaction that has seldom come to me in the doing of any other professional task. Here I was at last fighting for justice and for justice alone. There was no possibility of advantage to me; quite the contrary. It was a wonderful feeling and I fought like a tiger for that man. I got him off, too, but it was by a five-to-four vote in the Supreme Court, after two prolonged and interesting arguments. It was a close squeak, and the case made history, as it was the first time the Supreme Court had ever construed the provisions of the treason article of the Constitution; the first time a treason case had come before the court.

Think of the work of those devoted men and women who serve the poor in the Legal Aid Societies. Those cases do not get to the Supreme Court. They have to do with all the cunning ways in which the so-called "little people" are victimized by employers and landlords and the sellers of merchandise on conditional sales agreements, domestic difficulties, and what not. They become experts in all the odds and ends of the law with which the average lawyer has no concern and in the midst of which he would be bewildered. But the contribution to our society, to our beloved American democracy is indeed very great.

Another thing lawyers can do is become interested in Bar Association activities, and participate in the committee work which leads to improvements in the administration of justice. Unselfish, disinterested work of this kind is a great character builder. It gives our minds greater scope, extends our horizons, and makes us in every way better lawyers. But it is a mere waste of time to do these things in a perfunctory way, or to use them as a means of hobnobbing with judges and catering to the wishes of those in positions of power and influence. Remember, we are supposed to be in there fighting for justice, not appeasing and compromising on matters of principle in a scramble for some of the crumbs. So I would advise any lawyer to join up with the Section of Judicial Administration of the American Bar Association or the similar section or committee of his local State Bar Association and put his shoulder to the wheel.

And what is the judge's responsibility? When I started making speeches in favor of the minimum standards, I noticed that every time I hit a sore spot there was an immediate hue and cry: "Harold, why don't you mind your own business and stick to your cases in the courthouse, where you belong."

Nothing could be more unsound than this point of view. The judge's function goes far beyond the mere decision of the cases which come before him. He is the duly certified champion of justice and the people look to him for leadership in matters of improving the laws and bringing court procedures up-to-date. An experienced judge is supposed to know more about these things than anyone else and he speaks with authority. Moreover, the prime movers in such matters have traditionally been judges, including Chief Justice William Howard Taft, Chief Justice Charles Evans Hughes, Chief Justice Harlan Fiske Stone, and Chief Justice Fred M. Vinson, and a multitude of other state and federal jurists.

The idea that judges should stand aloof from such matters probably originated in the perfectly sound principle that it is undignified and at least in bad taste for judges to become involved in controversial matters, which in many instances are more or less likely to come before the judge for adjudication in some form later on. That is why it is generally so difficult to get a judge to make a good speech. Most of the subjects he is vitally interested in are taboo. But it is always proper and in good taste for a judge to discuss improvements in the administration of justice.

There are one or two other comments by way of footnotes, before I pass on to what the citizen may do. After all, my experience as a judge has only covered the brief space of seven years, and I am in no position to do more than reflect some of my own personal thoughts.

If the judge has constantly before him the realization that he is far from being the center of the universe and that he must seek guidance from Almighty God he is apt to keep pretty close to the ideal of justice. It is when he begins to throw his weight around that his judgments are apt to miss the mark. A corollary to this is that the judge must do his own job conscientiously according to his own lights and not keep worrying about whether or not the judges of some appellate court are going to agree with him. Once a trial judge or judge on an intermediate appellate court begins to try to figure out the personal philosophies and individual whimsies of the judges on the court just above him, he is bound to wind up in a fog.

Now we come to the person who may be the most important of the lot, the citizen. If we are to have one hundred percent justice, which is the only justice worth having, every single member of the community must make his individual contribution, and the opportunities to do so are legion.

The essential material without which courts cannot function at all is what we lawyers and judges call "the facts," and these "facts" are the conclusions drawn from evidence of happenings in the course of human affairs. The evidence generally consists of testimony by witnesses. And yet how often does a witness quietly slip away or affirmatively refuse to give his name or address, because he does not wish to be bothered going to court where he may have to submit to a very unpleasant cross-examination in the course of which his personal life may be open to scrutiny. Especially professional people often resent having to go to court as witnesses although the subject of their testimony may be an automobile accident or a business conversation or a robbery. And so principle number one is that perhaps the most important contribution to justice that any single member of society can make is to assist the search

132

for the truth by testifying in court to matters within his personal knowledge. One of the surest ways to sabotage justice is to sneak away and leave the field open for the unscrupulous to fill the gap.

Another soft spot is the tendency to avoid jury service or to fail to measure up to what is required of jurors when in attendance. A juror should feel the same sense of responsibility that a judge should have. One would suppose that the least a juror should do is to follow the instructions of the judge presiding over the case. And yet how often do jurors read the newspapers and listen to comment on the case over the radio or on television, despite the most explicit orders by the judge not to do so. How many jurors talk the case over with their wives or with their business associates while the case is still going on! And the books are full of instances where jurors have made little investigations of their own during court recesses. Basically all these matters come down to a sense of justice and fair play. It is the evidence produced in open court and known to all participants that is the material available for use by the court and jury alike; it is the views and arguments of the lawyers in the case and those of the other eleven jurors which are, according to law, entitled to affect the judgment of the juror in question in arriving at a verdict.

How wrong it is for jurors to decide a case according to whether they like the lawyer for one side or another, or on views of the law contradictory to those contained in the judge's instructions! I often wonder whether the oath to jurors is administered with sufficient ceremony and dignity. I have seen some judges charge a jury in such a fashion as to leave practically no impression upon them, while other judges take time and seem to have a genius for arousing in jurors a sense of responsibility and a sincere desire to do their very best to arrive at a just verdict.

Where majority verdicts are allowed, it is indispensable

133

that no verdict be arrived at without hearing and considering the views of each of the twelve jurors. Merely to take a vote and announce the result as soon as ten have agreed is likely to exclude entirely the point of view of the jurors who may have the most substantial contribution to make. The cross section of the community rule becomes meaningless mumbo jumbo if the representatives of minority groups are thus disregarded. And it is well to remember that we are all members of minority groups. In some communities it is the landlords or members of unions or bankers or drivers of Cadillac cars.

How about the reporters, editors, radio commentators, and journalists? Do they invariably make their proper contribution to the administration of justice, or do they more often than not muddy the waters with sensational stories about confessions which may never be received in evidence at the trial and an interesting catalogue of the defendant's prior convictions of crime, which everyone knows will not be admissible in evidence unless the defendant testifies in his own defense and submits himself to cross-examination? Is this sort of thing fair; is it justice?

One of the most unfortunate developments of these present troubled times is the fact that the average man in the street is apt to hold a personal grudge against the lawyer who defends someone charged with serious crime. Perhaps this has always been so to some extent; but it is all wrong. Everyone charged with crime is entitled to have a lawyer to defend him. And the more loathsome the crime the more important it is to us as a free nation to give the defendant the protection to which he is entitled according to law. We must find some way to make these things clear to the public at large.

The schoolteachers and the university professors also have much to contribute aside from the subject matter of the courses they teach. The Good Book says, "The letter killeth, but the spirit giveth life." And I wish to close with the same spiritual note I sounded in the beginning. There is a certain unity to the things of the spirit, they pervade everything and they should always be part and parcel of the daily work of our teachers.

Has it ever occurred to you that there is a connection between justice and good will and freedom? Each of these is an essentially spiritual force and each reacts on the other. None of the things I have been pressing upon your attention are possible except by the coöperation of large masses of people who trust one another, who wish one another well, and who respect the other person's point of view. Our teachers are supposed to try to give their pupils some understanding of the traditions of this great country of ours and the principles which lie behind our constitutions and our laws, aren't they? Of course they are! And this applies to all the teachers in one way or another. If so, I should like to inquire whether there are any principles more fundamental to American democracy than those I have just mentioned—justice, good will, and freedom?

Let others call us moneygrubbers and materialists or whatever they choose. So long as we cling to the principles of the founders the Republic is safe.

11 Guts and Loyalty

1956

Mr. J. Edgar Hoover, distinguished guests, and members of the FBI National Academy graduating class, I need not tell you that I am highly complimented by the invitation to make the commencement address here this morning. It is an honor and a privilege; and I shall try to discuss a few fundamentals in such fashion that they will stay with you over the years.

In a way I am today making a part payment on account of a debt of gratitude which I owe the FBI. I shall never forget those interminable nine months of the trial of the Communist leaders in 1949, when FBI men watched over me day and night. The two men assigned to protect me were Charlie Smith and George Sullivan, two of the nicest men I ever met in my life. They kept coming back every once in a while long after the trial was over. I never knew why they came or why they went but I was grateful. Even last June when I had a speaking engagement in El Paso, as Mrs. Medina and I got off the plane there were some FBI men ready to take over.

With these preliminaries, let us get down to business. Probably today the greatest problem which faces the nation on the domestic front is law enforcement. In my considered judgment the most significant development in law enforcement in the United States in my lifetime is the Federal Bureau of Investigation. The FBI has been extraordinarily fortunate in having as its executive head a man with the balance and the judgment and the vigor of J. Edgar Hoover. The reasons why law enforcement officers such as you do their work so well are that they are carefully selected, they are flexible, and have gone through the necessary discipline and training which leads to the ceremonies here this morning. The FBI National Academy is today an honored institution in the law enforcement profession of our nation. Another reason why law enforcement officers do their work well is that for the first time in the history of our nation, so far as I am aware, we have in the FBI National Academy a police training school which is wholly divorced from any sort of political interference, whether the Democrats are in power or the Republicans are in power.

The public confidence which the FBI enjoys is in no small measure due to the assurance which everyone feels that no one, and I mean absolutely no one, will interfere with it in the performance of its duties in the detection of crime and the apprehension of criminals. So far, so good. But there is another side to the picture, which I hope is equally clear both to you and to the public.

I used to teach at Columbia Law School. My classes always came from nine to ten in the morning and then I went downtown to my law practice and my court work. Suddenly, after about twenty-five years, it was discovered that I had some capacity as a jury lawyer. Well, these long complicated jury trials keep a man on the go practically twenty-four hours a day, as you men know only too well; and so I was obliged to give up my teaching. As I approached my last lecture, after a full twenty-five years at the school, I pondered and pondered as to what I could say, what I could leave with these boys and girls as the quintessence of what I had learned as a practicing lawyer. It was a solemn occasion for me; and I rather suspect

137

that those boys and girls just about to enter the legal profession remember even today the substance of my message.

What I said was something like this: You students have been working hard for three years of your law school course and are just about to graduate. Naturally, what has been uppermost in your minds during these three years has been getting good marks, standing as high in the class as you could, as everyone knows that the best jobs downtown go to those with the best scholastic records. But I tell you with all the earnestness at my command that brains are cheap. One can always hire some bright person to do a good technical job. Your progress at the Bar, the attainment of a position of leadership and influence among the lawyers of your time will depend upon guts and loyalty. And then I went on to give a number of examples which now I have mostly forgotten.

There is no point in my talking to you this morning about guts. You men have got the guts; and I could probably learn a lot from you on that subject. What a wonderful thing it is to be the kind of a man who will stick when the going is tough, the kind of a man a person in real bad trouble would like to have as a friend standing beside him as a strong, dependable, and absolutely fearless defender!

But the subject I really want to talk about this morning is loyalty. Some years ago, not long after the trial of the Communist leaders, I made a little speech to the Press Club in San Francisco. After my talk was over some of the men began asking questions. One of them was "Judge, how do you define loyalty?" Well, I had never thought about the subject in terms of a definition; and I said I did not know whether or not I could define it but I could tell them how you get that way. And I added, "A person who has good will and justice and freedom in his heart is bound to be loyal. He will be loyal to his friends and to his family and to the institutions of learning he attended, and to his religion, and to America, just as surely as the day follows the night."

For you loyalty does not mean marching around waving the American flag, although you as well as each and every one of the rest of us Americans honor and revere our country's flag. Whether you realize it or not, you will be among those few of the elect who will have constant opportunities, even from day to day, to protect our precious freedoms, the rights so plainly written in our Constitution, and to uphold the laws of the United States and our institutions. There will be temptations, almost daily, in your zeal to pursue the violators of our laws, to do things which will really undermine these laws.

Nothing bothers me quite so much as these statements the public prosecutors issue from time to time to the effect that in a certain period of time the particular prosecutor obtained a 99.75 percentage of convictions. Perhaps they do this for some sort of political preferment; perhaps it is a sort of boastfulness that is natural to almost all of us. But the inevitable impression made by statements of this kind is that the prosecutor is more interested in convictions than he is in justice and the integrity of the laws and the Constitution of the United States.

As you proceed with your work from this moment henceforth, I would have you always conscious of the fact that your first duty, above all others, is to maintain the integrity of our laws and our freedoms. No convictions based upon some violations of these laws or Constitutional rights can possibly benefit our nation in the long run.

Let me be specific. You know that the Constitution forbids unreasonable searches and seizures; you know that, however guilty a person may be, you have no right to enter premises or safe-deposit boxes without a search warrant duly obtained; you know that in the affidavits or petitions upon which such search warrants are procured, you must be scrupulously accurate and truthful in the statements you put in such affidavits and petitions; you know that all constitutional rights are inviolate, including the Fifth Amendment, against which there has been so much irresponsible public clamor; you know that

139

when a suspect is placed under arrest you are required without undue delay to bring the man before a judicial officer so that he may be admitted to bail and the charge against him may be known; you know that a man charged with crime is entitled to advice of counsel. What I wish to leave with you today is that all these and others are rights of an accused which come to us because men fought and struggled for freedom. Once lost, these precious freedoms are most difficult to regain; once whittled away or disregarded and neglected, they cease to be realities and vanish into thin air. You men stand at the first line of defense, and I would have you be constantly mindful of your trust.

My first real contact with the FBI was on the occasion during World War II when I was assigned as counsel, without compensation, to defend Anthony Cramer, a German-born American citizen charged with treason for having had some dealings with the saboteurs who landed on Long Island and in Florida from German submarines.

The part played by the FBI in the discovery and apprehension of each and every person implicated in that most serious enterprise, which was designed to cripple the American war effort through sabotage, was one of the brightest chapters in its history.

After Cramer's apprehension a number of FBI agents interviewed him and he made a series of statements. The contents of his room were taken into custody and a large amount of evidence at the trial derived from the documents and the articles found there. But he was at all times advised of his rights; the interrogation, while persistent and searching, was conducted in a reasonable and proper manner; there was nothing remotely approximating any third degree or any prolonged and unreasonable sessions; the procedure adopted prior to the searching of his room and taking into possession what was there was in strict compliance with the law; and, even as defense counsel, I was proud of the way FBI men conducted themselves, and I said so to the jury.

You men, who are about to carry these heavy burdens and responsibilities, go on your way with my blessings.

It is a pleasure to have been with you here this morning, and I thank you for listening to me.

12 Our Capacity for Growth

1952

In the span of my lifetime there has been a series of revolutions in education. Even in my youth, which after all was not so very long ago, Latin and Greek were the backbone of the course in liberal arts leading to the AB degree. And when, as a Junior, I elected to major in the Department of Modern Languages and Literatures there was none to challenge the view that the study of modern languages was important not merely to develop a speaking and reading knowledge of other languages, but more especially to learn the progress of ideas and the cultures of other places and civilizations. How easy it is to take what seems to be a "practical" view of things and miss the precious fundamentals which help us develop a true sense of human values.

As a matter of fact, our happiness as individuals, our success in life in the broadest sense of that much abused word "success" is bound to depend upon a just and sound appraisal of human values, and action from day to day in conformity with this appraisal.

Despite the fact that I devoted many years to the study of the classics and to the literature of France and Spain, it was not until I was well in my forties that I began to realize and appreciate the significance of one of the most important of all human capacities. This was brought home to me one Alumni Day at Princeton when as chairman of the committee it was my function to introduce John Foster Dulles as the principal speaker. He and I were boys together at Princeton just one year apart, and I have followed his career as he won distinction at the bar and gradually became more and more active in international affairs and in church affairs also. He is a perfect example of how a person can grow; the ceaseless use of his physical and intellectual equipment having made him more and more useful to society and culminating in his extraordinary achievement in the formulation and adoption of the peace treaty with Japan.

As a boy there was one part of the New Testament that I simply could not understand. It seemed fundamentally wrong and terribly unfair. I refer to the parable of the talents in the twenty-fifth chapter of the Gospel According to St. Matthew, in which the master was delighted with the two servants who had speculated with the money he had left with them and said to each, "Well done, thou good and faithful servant," but said to him who had hidden his one talent in the earth:

> Thou oughtest therefore to have put my money to the exchangers, and then at my coming I should have received mine own with usury.
>
> Take therefore the talent from him, and give it unto him which hath ten talents.
>
> For unto every one that hath shall be given, and he shall have abundance: but from him that hath not shall be taken away even that which he hath.
>
> And cast ye the unprofitable servant into utter darkness: there shall be weeping and gnashing of teeth.

This seems fundamentally wrong, doesn't it? And yet we know that Christ understood men better than anyone else

143

ever did. He always spoke with a certain mysticism, hiding his meaning in the parables which have come down to us. He knew what it was necessary for man to do in order to lead a happy, useful, abundant life. One is never wrong in following His precepts to the letter.

What He is telling us is—don't be afraid, don't be discouraged, don't be cynical, don't be lazy; but keep plugging away all the time with zest and enthusiasm.

Whether we like it or not the fact is that human nature stays just about the same over the centuries. What holds most of us back today is just what held people back two thousand years ago. Everyone seems to be looking for security. Boys just out of college ask personnel directors what the pension rights are and at what age they will be allowed to retire. Croakers abound everywhere telling us that everything is going to pot, that the world is plumb full of corruption, and that nothing can be done about it. But the truth is that this do-nothing policy of playing everything safe is just about the worst thing a person can do. When the parable says "from him that hath not shall be taken away even that which he hath" it is telling us what really happens. It is the reverse of the principle of the capacity for growth. It is an inevitable, inexorable law which inheres in our physical, mental, and psychological make-up as human beings.

When I was a boy in school one of the older students named Herb Bradley, who was quite an athlete and was then in the graduating class, came down to the gym one day and called us little fellows around him and he put out his hand and placed a fifty-cent piece on his finger tips. He held his hand out in front of us and that fifty-cent piece turned over and over until it reached his palm and then it turned over and over back again to the tips of his fingers. It seemed a perfectly miraculous thing. One could not observe the slightest movement of his hand and this performance greatly increased our admiration and respect for the performer. What had happened was that he had been practicing alone in his room for

144

about six months and had finally succeeded in getting such control of the tiny nerves and muscles in the palm of his hand that he could cause the fifty-cent piece to act in the way I have described.

And so it is with our minds and especially with those spiritual qualities which are sometimes described by the word "character." Self-control and what we often call guts are pretty important traits of character, and they can be developed and strengthened just as we can develop and strengthen our muscles.

From the day we are born until we are called into the great beyond there is never a day in which we stay quite the same as we were the day before. Changes go on continually; some for the better, some for the worse. We are supposed to use these capacities, to develop them; not to let them wither and become extinct.

How surprising it is to see, after the lapse of forty or fifty years, how some of the men in a college class who seemed to have such promise, who seemed destined to leadership and the accomplishment of great things which would have benefited their families, the community, and the nation, wind up without having done anything to speak of. On the other hand, some who seemed far less bright and far less capable wind up in the positions that you would have expected the others to have. Doubtless, different persons have different opportunities and the old adage that "nothing succeeds like success" really means that those who have the opportunity to develop their talents become more and more capable until they truly reach the heights. But it is my experience that hardly anyone goes through life without having had many opportunities which were permitted to pass by.

Moreover, the ten-talent man or woman may be making a significant contribution to society without any blowing of trumpets, without making a lot of money, and without having attained any high political or other offices. They have their reward and in this life too. The person who is constantly active, constantly accomplishing some good work, and hence constantly growing in every way is bound to be happy in his work. Melancholy thoughts and despondent introspection are not for him.

Some years ago when I was elected vice-president of the Class of 1909 of Princeton there seemed to be nothing for a vice-president to do and so I volunteered to write the obituary articles for publication in the *Alumni Weekly* when one or another of us was beckoned to what we call the Advance Guard. The first one had to do with a man named Pat LeFevre. I knew very little about him except that he was the principal of a high school in Dayton, Ohio. The busy days at the end of each school year in June had probably kept him away from our reunions. I started gathering material in my methodical way, writing to a lot of people, checking records and so on, and I discovered just the sort of person we are discussing today. He had started in teaching English, then he began working with the football team. Over the years he had influenced the lives of thousands of boys and girls. He had kept growing all the time. Sometimes in the middle of one of his classes he would lay aside the books and just talk for a while, saying the most unforgettable things which burned themselves into the souls of those who listened. Sometimes he would do this between the halves of a football game. None knew when he might hold forth. And from day to day, in and out of school his example and the radiance of his personality were at work. When he died it seemed as though all Dayton came out to the funeral.

He was not the president of a bank or a famous professor in some institution of learning or President of the United States —but he was a ten-talent man who had heeded the words of the parable. He had met every test, without fuss or flurry, just plugging away from day to day. How full of meaning are those words, "By their fruits shall ye know them."

13 Security

1953

There is no security in material things; it is mere illusion to suppose that one can purchase security or attain it otherwise than by the development of our personal resources as individual human beings. The most valuable and precious things in life cannot be bought by money. Security is one of these.

With the passage of years most of us come to perceive certain significant trends in the course of human affairs. Things we had been taught in our youth, bits of history, and patterns of behavior seem to take on a new significance. I well remember the day when, only a few years ago, I was reading a book on the history of philosophy. Each new philosopher down through the ages seemed to be inventing a new terminology and the classification of groups and schools was bewildering. It all seemed so unnecessary and egotistical. Then the thought occurred to me that perhaps from one age to another the problems were different and that underneath these changes of terminology and descriptions of the different philosophical doctrines there was a groping for some solution of the particular, current problems with which mankind was faced, as one school of philosophers succeeded another. However that

147

may be, it is clear to me that people all over the world in the last few years have developed an almost morbid interest in security. Surely there is nothing strange about this when we consider what has been happening during the lives of even the youngest among us today.

I was talking recently with a man in charge of the personnel division of one of the large manufacturing concerns and he told me as the young men just out of college applied for their jobs a good many of them seemed especially interested in the age of retirement, the pension rights, and matters of that sort. Young girls are hardly out of the church where the wedding ceremony is performed when they permit their thoughts to wander to the subject of when their husbands, who are around twenty-one or twenty-two, are going to retire so that they may spend the rest of their lives basking in the sunshine, traveling around the world, and seeing all the sights. They also seem to think of the possibility that the young man whom they have just married may die and it is not long before they start picking on him to take out enough insurance to leave them and the offspring on easy street.

What few people seem to realize is that practically everybody gets most of his fun out of his work. This basking in the sunshine and sitting around reading all the new novels and detective stories as they come out is a good thing to talk about when you are selling life insurance; but for most of us it just does not work.

For professional men such as architects, engineers, lawyers, doctors, and so on, the proposition is almost self-evident. Think of the thrill that must come to a young surgeon as he begins to master the special skills and techniques of his profession. The sense of power and achievement and the continuous growth which only experience and application can bring about lead him on, as it were, from one adventure to another.

Picture in your minds the lawyer preparing for the cross-examination of some utterly unscrupulous person of excep-

148

tional intelligence who is playing for high stakes and who has developed a pat story which covers every phase of the transaction involved in some court proceeding. The task of mastering all the intricate details, studying the personal traits of the witness and of the jurors and of the judge, and then planning a series of questions to break the witness and lay bare the truth is just about as exciting and stirring an experience as one could well imagine. The subtlety of it, the infinite variety of forces, great and small, which affect human beings as they prey upon one another either in the marts of trade or the pursuit of criminal purposes call for the highest quality of imaginative work, great flexibility of mind, and tenacity of purpose.

But the same principle applies to people in every walk of life whatever their employment or their trade or occupation. Superficially, it looks as though the engineers and the chemists and the infinite variety of research workers had the best of it. But nothing pleases me so much as to talk to a carpenter or a fisherman about the details of his work. I remember once sitting around in Harwich Port on Cape Cod talking with the men who were getting their gear ready for an early start the next morning for the fishing grounds. There is always just the right way to set a hook, just the right way to put on the bait, and just the right way to do an infinite amount of other little things that seem to the rest of us to be merely routine, except that when we try to do any one of them we always seem to have a special knack for doing it wrong.

Some years ago I had a bay man working for me on Long Island named John Raynor. Every once in a while we used to go off the beach in a dory to do some fishing. As we stood there on the beach I could not see how we could ever get the little dory out through the breakers. They came in one on top of another and I was sure we would be swamped. But he stood there calmly watching the waves for perhaps two or three minutes and then he would say, "Here we go," and we would push the dory out into the ocean, hop in, and we were off. The first thing I knew we were out beyond the breakers and not one of them had come anywhere near us. His skill and experience were such that he could tell the sequence of the waves and he knew just the instant of time when conditions were exactly right for that little trip of four or five hundred yards through what appeared to be a mass of white water.

One of the things that really makes hard work for students is the way literary figures put pepper and salt in their work by using words which represent the special terminology of masons or painters or textile workers or what not. When you are translating from French or German or any other language it is a baffling task to do any sort of job of rendering into English the work of some master craftsman when the dictionary turns up a series of words the meaning of which remains completely obscure. But they all do it and it works. This sort of thing adds character and finish to a piece of literature and I ask you to reflect upon the satisfaction which must come to those who coin and use these special words. Everyone likes to spread an air of mystery about his skills. People complain about the doctors writing their prescriptions for aspirin and bicarbonate of soda in Latin; and the lawyers are supposed to have developed a special jargon to mystify the population in general and increase the size of their fees. But I tell you that this is just one of the ways used from the dawn of history by the human animal for his own pleasure and gratification. That is one of the ways we all have fun. And, incidentally, it is one of the reasons why it is so difficult to get the children of those who live in homes where a foreign language is spoken to master the English language and stand forth as little Americans rather than as little Italians or little Puerto Ricans. They simply cannot resist the advantage they have over the other little boys and girls in school and on the streets when they use words and converse in a tongue which the others do not understand.

The man who runs my boat has a tricky way of adjusting the barometer so that no one else can tell whether it has been going up or down; he coils the ropes in a special way so that anyone else trying to manipulate them will get them in a mess; he operates the clutches, the starting apparatus, and everything else by levers that he hides away, as well as he can, so that even a close observer will be mystified by the way the boat glides into the smallest space with an eggshell landing.

Perhaps you have read some of the writings of the great entomologist, Jean Henri Fabre. The infinite patience with which he observed the conduct of the bees and wasps and beetles and caterpillars is simply out of this world. I suppose few men got as much fun out of life as he did; and he had the genius to write about his work in an interesting way and at the same time give us an insight into some of the problems of human behavior that has been most revealing.

By way of contrast, I tried one of these Wage and Hour cases a few years ago. It involved the classifications of the workers in the RCA plant at Camden, New Jersey. One would suppose that a case of this sort would be as dry as dust, but it wasn't. You should have heard some of those men telling me about capacitors and transformers and the way they processed the work in the plant so that each individual operation might be done with the greatest economy in the use of time and materials. One of the men had received several increases in pay for improvements that he had developed and I can still see the flush on his cheek and the sparkle in his eye as he told me about them.

Just compare these things with sitting around living the life of Reilly and basking in the sunshine while all your innate talents gradually wither and disappear, and all that remains is the veneer and polish which comes with the life of leisure.

And so I tell you, don't let anybody fool you about this retirement business and sitting around taking it easy. The happiness in life for you lies in the mastery of the field in which you choose to work. Constant thought, and the exercise of your imagination, the strengthening of your character by determination to overcome obstacles which seem insurmountable —these are the things that will constitute your real security.

Just about the worst thing the average man or woman can do is to get in the frame of mind where he or she is thinking all the time about security. It is just like taking dope. If you keep thinking about security long enough, especially when you are under fifty, you begin to live in a topsy-turvy world. You come to think about things as fun which are really not fun at all, and you wind up leading a more or less wretched existence all the while telling yourself what a gorgeous time you are having, without really believing it.

Now I return to the point at which I started this little argument. In the lives of each of us, as in the role of humanity in history, there is a time for everything. Probably many of you have read Cicero's *De Senectute*, his charming little essay on old age. We will probably have to revise his description of the various periods in the life of man, as those whom he considered in old age are nowadays just about getting into their stride. But the principle is the same. He tells us that the way to live a rich, useful, and happy life is to do at each stage of our existence the things that are appropriate and fitting to the particular period in which we find ourselves at any given moment.

It is proper and fitting that one should slow up a bit, drop into a canter after the race is run, as old Justice Holmes said in that wonderful talk over the radio when he was just past ninety; but the life full of effort and striving is the life that develops our abilities and our character to their true potential. This only is true success and it brings the only true security.

14 In Litteris Libertas

1958

President Kirk, Mr. Barrett, each and every one of that devoted band of administrators on the staff of the Columbia Libraries from the top down, Friends of the Columbia Libraries, and all others gathered together here this evening to assist in making this Bicentennial Anniversary a memorable one:

It is fitting that Columbia should not permit this significant occasion to pass without appropriate ceremonies to mark the passage of the first two hundred years of the existence of what is now without a doubt the nerve center of the principal activities of this great university—education and research. It is fitting not only because in a country so young as the United States of America the passage of so long a time betokens a certain permanence, giving assurance of solid accomplishment, but also because we are now in a world of turmoil and unrest, intolerance and subversion, where tyranny rules supreme over vast reaches of the earth and institutions such as the Columbia Libraries stand out as beacons to light the way to freedom for generations in the time to come. I would emphasize at the outset that freedom and the liberal arts go hand

153

and hand. And so I have chosen as the title of this address, *"In Litteris Libertas."* However I may seem to wander here and there I hope you may feel the play of this melody throughout —the libraries as beacons of freedom, leading us on to the pursuit of knowledge through the inviting highways and by-paths of the liberal arts. And I would also sound a note to remind us of Columbia as a treasure house of things peculiarly representative of the American scene and of our beloved City of New York.

One of the favorite rhetorical devices of our old friend Marcus Tullius Cicero was the *praeteritio.* He would say, in effect, "I pass by this or that," but in doing so he brought pleasure to those who heard him by the interesting matter in his seeming digressions, while at the same time driving his main theme home, on the bias, as it were. So we turn to digression number one.

With fire, flood, and hurricanes, to say nothing of the carelessness and destructiveness of mankind in general, it seems almost a miracle that any of the priceless original books of centuries ago should still survive, with their artistic embellishments of illustration, illumination, bindings and exquisite papyrus, vellum, paper, and miscellaneous fittings. I need not refer to the effect of the bombing of Cassino and of London and a host of other places in the recent war or of the atom bombs and intercontinental missiles of the future that we hear so much about. I remember once reading in Hazlitt's *History of the Venetian Republic* how Petrarch, who had a marvelous collection of medieval books and manuscripts, "was in perpetual dread of losing his treasures by some unlucky fire, by damp, or by dry-rot." So he gave the collection to the Republic. But after a hundred years or so all were gone, except a half-dozen items, including a twelfth-century French missal. Think of the wilful, criminal destruction of the archives of the churches and monasteries and of many civil establishments in Cromwell's time. I had a taste of this sort of thing myself when my library at Westhampton, Long Island, with

154

all my notes and memoranda and even a few incunabula, was washed away in the hurricane of September 21, 1938.

On the other hand, there has always been a sturdy and sizable band of preservers, who quietly hide and protect all sorts of things for posterity: books, diaries, letters, and everything else under the sun. Only the other day Elizabeth Trotter of Philadelphia, my wife's cousin, sent several boxes full of letters, genealogical data, and newspapers, including contemporary descriptions of the Burr-Hamilton affair, all connected in some way with a certain Standish Forde of Philadelphia. My wife's middle name is Forde, one of our sons is Standish Forde and one of our grandsons bears the same name. A summer or two ago we were invited to dine at Sylvester Manor on Shelter Island by "the Lord of the Manor," Andrew Fiske, and his lovely wife. Before I knew it he had taken me aside, opened a huge wall safe as large as a good-sized room, and we were soon poring over some of the most interesting original letters I have ever read, all written, as I recall, during or shortly after the Revolution. This is the stuff out of which true history is distilled. The quantity still in private hands and subject to all sorts of risks of mutilation or destruction is incalculable, but undoubtedly very large. The point I would make in passing is that each and every such item belongs in some great public institution such as the Columbia Libraries, where the letters or journals or whatnot else can be preserved intact, catalogued, and, on appropriate occasions and under proper safeguards, displayed.

Now for digression number two. I often wonder how many ordinarily well-informed and intelligent people have any conception of the current day-to-day problems with which the Columbia Libraries are faced. Let us assume, as I hinted a moment ago, that our principal duties are to gather together and make available to faculty and students and perhaps to scholars generally the books and allied materials indispensable to the processes and procedures of education and research. Forget the Rare Books and Special Col-

155

lections, to which I shall return. I hope a few statistics will not bore you. Here they are. The Columbia Libraries serve the needs of some 27,000 students and over 4,000 faculty members. It is anticipated that by 1970 the enrollment will have increased by from 2,700 to 5,400 additional students. At Columbia it is possible to take courses in forty-one different languages; the undergraduate programs, the professional schools, and the graduate faculties offer opportunities leading to forty-nine different degrees, and almost 5,000 different courses.

By 1870, there were in the Columbia Libraries 14,100 volumes; by 1897, 75,000 volumes; by 1931, 1,250,000 volumes; and by 1957, 2,900,000 volumes, with an insurance value of $20,000,000.

The current annual expense to Columbia University for the acquisition and preservation of library materials, for the staff members to provide circulation and reference services and to perform the operations connected with book orders, cataloguing, and binding has mounted to the incredible figure of $1,500,000.

Here is a partial but fairly complete list of the Columbia Libraries:

Avery Library of Architecture
Barnard College Library
Burgess Library (Social Sciences)
Carpenter Library (English and Modern Languages)
East Asiatic Library
Engineering Library
Geology Library
Greek and Latin Classics Library
Library of Business and Economics
Library of Chemistry and Chemical Engineering
Library of Columbia College
Library of Fine Arts
Library of Law and International Law

Library of Physics
Library of Plastic Surgery
Library of the School of Library Service
Library of Zoology and Botany
Mathematics Library
Medical Library
Music Library
Paterno Library
Philosophy Library
Psychology Library
Rare Books and Special Collections
School of Journalism Library
School of Pharmacy Library
Teachers College Library
Ware Collection

How is it possible to keep this huge congeries of libraries up-to-date, to ascertain and fill gaps in the collections of books in this field or that? The modern output of scientific books and periodicals all over the world presents a special problem. In the central clearinghouse section which receives, checks in, and distributes to the various university libraries the periodicals received from day to day it hardly seems possible, but the fact is that during the past year 110,000 items were processed. Government and foundation grants and projects present a very pressing library problem.

Nor does any department of this great university stand still. There are plans for a new Engineering Center, a proposed Fine Arts Center, a new Law Center, perhaps a branch library of the Geology Library to be established at or near the Lamont Geological Observatory at Palisades, New York, and so on. Some of these plans are soon to be put into effect, others are nebulous and in the early stages; and they all have to do in one way or another with books and library facilities.

Now, what is digression number two put in for? Well, I want you to see the problems for one thing. The modern demands for service seem impossible of fulfillment, the complexity of the task is baffling; but Columbia accepts the challenge and I have no fear of the outcome. For the goal toward which we eagerly press is worth all the effort and all the sacrifice. We must maintain free access to ideas, to new creative thought, and the unfettered functioning of the mind. Here in these hallowed walls we do not walk the chalk line of conformity, we do not think what we are told to think and stop there; fostered by the spirit of the liberal arts we reach out and probe to solve the secrets of the nature of man and of the cosmos. These Columbia Libraries are meant for the use of a free and independent people.

So much for the *praeteritio*. Now we turn directly to the task in hand.

Why are we gathered here in the year of our Lord 1958 to

celebrate the founding of the Columbia Libraries? Beginnings are always interesting and significant. The earliest acquisition was a bequest by the Honorable Joseph Murray, Esquire, of the Middle Temple, according to his bookplate; one of the governors of the College, a member of his Majesty's Council for the Province of New York, and "the most considerable Lawyer here in his time." He died in April, 1757, and left his residuary estate "including a fine library" to "the Governors of the College of the Province of New York, by whatever name they are called." It is not known exactly when the books were handed over, but this gift was supplemented by another bequest from the Reverend Duncombe Bristowe, D.D., a graduate of Brasenose College, Oxford, and Rector of Allhallows, Staining within Aldgate, London, who died in June, 1758. The Reverend Dr. Bristowe made the bequest to the Society for the Propagation of the Gospel "to be sent to the College of New York, of which Dr. Johnson is President, or to such Place or Places as the Society should direct." Some of these books "are adorned with the bookplate of the Rev. Dr. Duncombe Bristowe, as also with the ancient emblem of the Venerable Society for the Propagation of the Gospel in Foreign Parts."

And so the Columbia Libraries were born. These precious volumes were used to good purpose by the little band of educators who then made up the College, but storms were brewing, and in April and May of 1776 the College building was given up to the patriot troops and the books and apparatus removed to the City Hall, where the British and Hessian soldiers played havoc with them soon after General Howe's entry into New York in September, 1776. Some of them were deposited in a closet near the organ loft in St. Paul's and rumor had it that many were protected in a stoned-up doorway where they were found in 1802 by some workmen employed in preparing a place for the organ. An interesting item in the *Morning Chronicle* on December 18, 1802, branded this as a hoax "invented by some wag," and added: "The report had gained so much by travelling that it was said a librarian was discovered with the library, who, on coming out into the city, was quite surprised with the changes that had taken place."

President Butler once reported that the minutes of the trustees disclosed the following library expenditures: for 1825, $177.44; 1827, $44.57; 1832, $51.75; 1843, $100; 1851, $400; 1862, $500.

From this brief historical recital I turn to a subject that will bring us back to our original theme. Most of us here tonight have probably been bitten by the book bug from early childhood. Even today it is only with a supreme effort that I pass one of the old-book stalls; they simply fascinate me. What pure delight it must be to spend one's days as Mr. Baughman does, examining the special gifts as they come in, plotting and scheming to get them, and then arranging them for study by historical or other scholars or for exhibition. He has the best job in the Libraries, I think.

Some of the recent acquisitions by the Columbia Libraries fit in exactly with what I am trying to say this evening. And, really, part of the celebration centers around the famous John Jay Collection, which a group of generous members of the Friends of the Columbia Libraries and their collaborators brought in last year. I am saving that for the end.

Also last year the Columbia Libraries received the Dr. Benjamin Salzer Collection of Mayor's Court Papers, about two thousand pieces in all, extending in date from 1681 to 1819. The history of this court goes back to 1650, when the States General ordered the establishment in New Amsterdam of a court similar to that in existence in the mother city. When the English conquered New Netherland in 1664, the name of this court of burgomasters and schepens was changed to the Mayor's Court and its development followed that of the English Mayor's Courts, notably that of the Lord Mayor of Lon-

159

don. The Salzer Collection also contains a large amount of material of the Court of General Sessions, relating to criminal matters.

Then, in browsing around, I came across two of George Washington's Manuscript Diaries for the year 1795, his last year but one as the first President of the United States, and 1798, the year before he died. These were presented to the University in 1951 by Charles Moran, Jr., a Columbia alumnus, by whose family they had been preserved and passed on from generation to generation since 1827.

One of the entries is on February 12, 1798, when he went "with the family" to a Ball in Alexandria "given by the Citizens of it & its vicinity in commemoration of the anniversary of my birthday." This came as quite a surprise, as most of us think of Washington's birthday as February 22. But it turned out that Alexandria was still using the old style calendar in 1798, which accounts for the difference of ten days. Really the change was one of eleven days, but we shall not pause to go into this. And, incidentally, those of us who love Alexandria and the people who live there recognize in this lack of the customary zeal to keep up with the times, this unwillingness to be hurried into new-fangled notions under the guise of progress one of the reasons Alexandria is so attractive and alluring.

But by far the most important acquisition by the Columbia Libraries for many a year is the John Jay Collection, which includes nearly two thousand pieces to and from more than two hundred and fifty individuals, including John Adams, Benjamin Franklin, Alexander Hamilton, Thomas Jefferson, John Paul Jones, Rufus King, the Marquis de Lafayette, Gouverneur Morris, General Schuyler, and George Washington. It is a veritable treasure house. Many of the most interesting items are on display here in Butler Library this evening, as you have doubtless already noticed.

How strange it is that so many of us here at Columbia know so little of the true stature and the outstanding accomplish-

160

ments of this great American patriot, one of Columbia's most illustrious sons. We pass by John Jay Hall, some of us almost every day of our lives, and probably even those familiar with the works of his early biographers think of him as cold and austere, more mind than man. And he was reserved, one of New York's aristocrats. But there were few who rendered such conspicuous, continuous, and unselfish services to America during the period of the Revolution, and before and after. Frank Monahan's *John Jay, Defender of Liberty* gives us a true measure of his greatness, and the title page displays this interesting summary:

Defender of Liberty against Kings & Peoples; Author of the Constitution & Governor of New York; President of the Continental Congress; Co-author of the Federalist; Negotiator of the Peace of 1783 & the Jay Treaty of 1794; First Chief Justice of the United States.

He loved Columbia too, taking his B.A. degree in the then King's College in 1764 and his M.A. degree in 1767. His son Peter Augustus Jay also received a B.A. degree in 1794, an M.A. in 1797 in what by that time had become Columbia College, and an honorary LL.D. in 1835.

But the man who smiles out to us from this fine collection is no austere and forbidding intellectual machine, but rather a hearty human being full of the zest of life, who was not only trusted and consulted on matters of the highest consequence in the affairs of government but was truly loved by such men as Washington, John Adams, and Hamilton, and a host of others. He had courage and he had that most rare of qualities, a serene outlook on men and events which made it possible for him to weather in silence and peace of mind many an unfounded personal attack upon his integrity, and many an unexpected and disappointing turn of events. In all this his absolute and unwavering faith in Christ as our Redeemer and our Saviour was a supreme resource. History has done him something less than justice.

It is not always easy to prove a point by reference to two or three out of two thousand pieces of a collection such as the John Jay papers, but I shall try.

What first caught my eye was a letter from John Adams, dated at Amsterdam, November 28, 1781. He is gloating over the capture of Cornwallis at Yorktown and is riding high, having been visited by a number of persons of consequence to offer congratulations. But he adds:

—but there are invisible FAIRIES who disconcert in the NIGHT
all the operations of the patriot in the Day.

Who of us has not been visited by these same FAIRIES!

There is a precious holographic letter written to Jay also by John Adams. John Adams is bowing out as the second President of the United States, to be succeeded, as it turned out, by Thomas Jefferson. Jay is serving his second term as governor of New York.

Washington November 24, 1800

Dear Sir

I received last week your friendly private Letter of the tenth. The assurance of the continuance of your friendship was unnecessary for me, because I have never had a doubt of it. But others invent and report as they please. They have presumed hitherto however more delicacy towards the friendship between you and me than any other.

The last Mission to France, and the consequent dismission of the twelve Regiments, although an essential branch of my System of Policy, has been to those who have been intriguing and laboring for an Army of fifty thousand Men, an unpardonable fault. If by their folly they have thrown themselves on their backs and Jacobins should walk over their bellies, as military Gentlemen express promotions over their heads, who should they blame but themselves?

Among the very few Truths in a late Pamphlet there is one that I shall ever acknowledge with pleasure, viz. that the principal Merit of the negotiations for Peace was Mr. Jays. I wish you would permit our Historical Society to print the Papers you drew up on that Occasion.

I often say that when my Confidence in Mr. Jay shall cease, I must give up the cause of Confidence and renounce it with all Men.

With great Truth and regard I am now and ever shall be your friend and humble servant.

John Adams

I have saved for the last the piece I like best. Jay and his wife, Sally Livingston Jay, sailed from the neighborhood of Philadelphia for Spain on October 20, 1779. This turned out to be one of his most unhappy and frustrating experiences. Mrs. Jay had requested General St. Clair to ask Washington for a lock of his hair so that she might take it with her as a keepsake. The lock of hair arrived with the following, entirely in Washington's own hand:

General Washington presents his most respectful compliments to Mrs. Jay—Honoured in her request by General St. Clair, he takes pleasure in presenting the inclosed, with thanks for so polite a testimony of her approbation & esteem —He wishes most fervently, that prosperous gales—an unruffled sea—& everything pleasing & desirable, may smooth the path she is about to walk in—

West-Point October 7th 1779

Yes, the Columbia Libraries and those of her sister universities and colleges are beacons of freedom beckoning to all who toil in the quest for truth and knowledge. Every branch of learning is solidly represented, and all, including those who seek some special proficiency as in medicine or the law or journalism or music, are enriched by the culture of the liberal arts, so indispensable to the development of creative thought and what we call, for lack of a better word, imagination. All who enter here may seek solace and refreshment in the delights of literature and the manifold allurements of the humanities. Here the sciences and the humanities walk together *pari passu*. Here no tyrant tells us what to learn or what to teach. And we pay a proper tribute to our forebears and to those who fought for freedom and made all these things possible. These are the thoughts I would have you associate with the celebration, on this 28th day of January in the year of our Lord 1958, of the Bicentennial Anniversary of the Founding of the Columbia Libraries. As John Jay would have said: for all these blessings we thank Almighty God, the creator and preserver of all mankind.

15 The Education of a Judge

1952

Over the years it has been borne in on me more and more that the administration of American justice cannot properly perform its function without mutual understanding, mutual confidence, and a real and lasting brotherhood as between the judges on one hand and the lawyers on the other.

So that you may follow me in my meandering ways I tell you now that my thread or motif, the melody, as it were, which will beat upon your ears now low and almost inaudible and now loud and clear, will be the human element in law. And bear in mind that the administration of justice is a great coöperative effort in which all the members of the community play their several and individual parts; some as judges; some as lawyers; some as jurors, witnesses, or citizens; who participate, to the extent of their various opportunities, in public affairs and in loyal service to their country.

I am what the university professors call a humanist, and a humanist is simply a person interested in the study of the human animal from every angle in order to distill out of such study a sound and proper sense of values. A man or woman who succeeds in this quest will, as an inevitable consequence, lead a useful, happy life even in the midst of hardships and difficulties such as would make others quite miserable. And the contrary is true. The man or woman who has a false or distorted sense of human values will never lead a useful, happy life even though possessed of fabulous wealth and material comforts of every name and description.

This is a funny world. Just as you think you are beginning to understand something you find that you are all wrong and that you have to start over again. And so I am going to give you some illustrations from my own experience to demonstrate that each of us has a lot to learn, and that the process of education, which begins when we are born, never ceases until the last call.

I never thought I knew so much law as on the day I graduated from law school. How merciful the good Lord is! It would have been most discouraging and disheartening had I then had the slightest inkling of how little I really did know about the law or anything else.

When, suddenly and unexpectedly, I learned that I might be appointed as a United States District Judge it seemed to me that I had always wanted to be a judge and that this would be the attainment of an ambition cherished since I was a child. But one day a reporter came in and asked me if I could tell him when it was that I first got the idea that I wanted to be a judge. After a little reflection I was able to tell him. The incident may furnish some interesting background.

As a young man in my twenties I used to argue a good many appeals in negligence cases and what we New Yorkers call nonenumerated motions, that is to say, appeals from interlocutory orders relating to various procedural matters, in the courtroom of the Appellate Division of the Supreme Court, First Department, which is located in the Appellate Division Courthouse on Madison Avenue and Twenty-fifth Street in New York City. One day as I sat in this courtroom waiting for my case to be called, I looked up and saw around the base of the huge glass dome over the courtroom the names of the judges who had sat in that court from the time it was established in 1896; and I saw on the walls and on easels portraits of the distinguished presiding justices who had served there over the years. There was something solemn and impressive about that courtroom, something symbolic of the dignity and of the eternal quality of the law with all its changes and adjustments. I saw more clearly the vision of the function of the administration of justice as the preserver of our American democracy and of our precious liberties and institutions. And lo the spark was fired and from that moment on through the balance of an active and busy career as a practicing lawyer I never ceased to hope that somehow, someday, I might become a judge.

Since I have been on the bench I have learned a lot. In the first place I learned a lot about myself as is shown by what I have just said. One of the most important of all the lessons I learned was the lesson of humility. I have never been of a meek or introspective bent of mind. In fact just the opposite. I have always loved a fight and took a lot of lickings, which didn't do me any harm. But this job of being a judge changes a man. It is an awesome thing to mete out justice. Inevitably one finds himself face to face with forces too great and too complicated to justify any belief that they may be surmounted by mere rationalization and study. The Good Book says that the letter killeth but the spirit giveth life. And don't forget that a judge sits there day in and day out under the shadow of our country's flag. This really does something to you. Above all it teaches humility, the greatest quality any judge can have. And pretty soon you find yourself just trying to administer the law as it should be administered and not giving a continental what anyone else may think even if this someone else happens to sit on a higher court. The responsibility of the trial judge is his own responsibility. If he really does the best he can, he has done all that the community has a right to expect of him. It is silly for him to try to figure out what someone else will think is the best he could have done. Please do not misunderstand me. I do not say that trial judges or any judges may blandly disregard the law as settled by precedents which they must follow. I refer to this business of trying to guess at the slant a higher court may take on open, controversial issues. It is futile to avoid one's own responsibility by trying to study the personalities and individual philosophies of the judges of some court to which appeals will lie from one's own judgments.

When I was in college I read one of the great books of all time, Victor Hugo's *Notre Dame de Paris,* the English title of which is sometimes given as *The Hunchback of Notre Dame.* I once wrote a thesis on that book and in it I stressed the artistry with which Victor Hugo had put together a series of characters in each of which there was some predominant human trait which could be turned to a good or an evil purpose. When studied with care the book revealed one of the most important lessons a human being can learn: and that is that each human quality is like a two-edged sword. The bright boy, for example, is apt to become indolent and careless and never amount to anything; a nervous, excitable person capable of significant creative effort may, because of lack of control or because of environment or for some other reason, waste his life in futile, undisciplined effort. Of course, the characteristics developed by Victor Hugo were not so simple and the results were tragic in the extreme; but I am not now engaged in literary criticism and exposition but sketching background.

There was one thing I learned the first day I sat on the bench. During my many years of practice I had reached the conclusion that there was nothing quite so bad as a judge who keeps talking all the time. I said to myself, "Why doesn't the old buzzard keep his mouth shut and let us lawyers try the case?" So when I became a judge I resolved that silence should be my motto.

I started in on my first assignment which was to the Motion Term. In the Southern District of New York this is a perfect

168

nightmare. The motions pile up and it sometimes takes many weeks to decide them all. Anyway, I sat there listening and it soon became apparent to see that this silence business was simply not for me. I had to make my choice. Either I was going to be a faker and play the part of someone else or I was going to be Harold Medina and do a certain amount of talking. So my resolution about silence went out the window.

And what was the result? At the beginning of every court day fixed for the hearing of contested motions we swear in a batch of attorneys to be admitted to practice in our district. I used to lean back and make a little speech. Sounds crazy, doesn't it? With a crowded calendar and a roomful of busy lawyers waiting to be reached for argument, why waste time?

But let me explain what I said to them and why I said it. I am very grateful to my profession and I desire in every way in my power to show my gratitude by helping the lawyers and by encouraging close and intimate relationship between the Bench and Bar. To swear in a group of lawyers without any semblance of ceremony seems to me to be a mistake; and I tried to add a certain dignity to the occasion and to do so in a way that would give it less the appearance of a purely perfunctory and meaningless performance. And so I used to mention, very briefly, the two things which I thought lawyers should most particularly keep in mind. The first is to eliminate this continual cussing out of the lawyer on the other side. One hardly ever goes through the argument of a motion or the trial of a case without a number of these nasty recriminations. As far as I can tell, they never help the lawyer who makes them and they go far to disturb the solidarity of the Bar and that feeling of brotherhood which is so essential to the administration of justice. The other point I made is that the lawyer must never forget that he is part of the administration of justice and that it is his duty at all times to help the court. Here again, a strict and persistent adherence to this simple and fundamental rule will do much to bring the Bench and Bar closer together.

169

And so I went on in my work from day to day asking questions, bedeviling the lawyers, and refusing to take submissions of even the most trivial motions. In this way I thought I got to the bottom of things more quickly. In any event, my whole life has been spent in argument and colloquy. It stimulates my thinking processes. After all, judges are not run in a mold and each man must bring to the bench his own peculiar talents and his own particular personality.

But this is something for me to watch out for, isn't it? I can see now that this talking business is going to be a real problem for me. Sometimes it is a good thing for the judge to speak up; more often it is better for him to listen.

So much for part one, illustrative of just a few of the things I have learned about myself.

The second thing I learned in the process of my education as a judge was that in the course of human affairs there are no absolutes. Beware of the man or woman with a will of adamant who says: "I will never do thus and so," and sticks to it despite unforeseen developments and further enlightenment. Consistency is not always a virtue.

When I was a young man at the Bar kicking around the courts or getting kicked around, which was more usually the case, I noticed that there was a certain phrase that judges used continually. It was "Counselor, I have your point. I'll take the papers." At first I thought these were words of encouragement; but I soon discovered that this was my cue to sit down. It was perfectly obvious that there had been no time to understand the matter I was there to argue. It was apparent to me that the judge had no opportunity to get my point; and I don't mind saying that nothing ever irritated me quite so much as the judge who was unwilling to listen. It seemed to me that this was the very thing the judge was paid to do; that it was discourteous and, particularly with the younger members of the Bar, discouraging and disheartening.

And so, as I approached my judicial duties I made up my

mind that this was one thing that I would certainly never do. On the contrary, I would listen to the lawyers till the cows came home and make sure that I understood all their points, however minute and apparently lacking in substance.

Accordingly, the first job assigned to me after I was sworn in on July 1st, 1947, was that of an assignment in the Motion Term. The first day of motions started in at ten-thirty o'clock in the morning and I listened and I listened until finally at six-thirty o'clock in the afternoon the last lawyer was through and I went home. "Well," said I, "this is not so bad." The second day, however, was quite a shock. I stayed there, with an hour's interval for lunch and another for supper, listening to arguments from ten-thirty in the morning until half-past eleven o'clock at night. I was so tired that I could hardly get off the bench and I had to get one of the lawyers to drive me home.

It may be that the lawyers we have in New York are different, more verbose and more persistent; but I am inclined to think that lawyers are the same the world over. They repeat and repeat—dash off into a digression here and a digression there. How they love to praise their clients, particularly if the client is sitting in the back of the courtroom and is in a position to pay a good fee.

Anyway, the result is that I now know it is absolutely impossible to listen to the lawyers until the cows come home, at least if you want to preserve your health. Doubtless there is a happy medium; and I hope with a few years of additional experience to find out just where the line should be drawn. So far I have never said, "Counselor, I have your point. I'll take the papers," when in truth and in fact I had no idea whatever what his point was. But you can depend on it, that day will come just as sure as the sunrise. I shall hate myself for it; I shall wish that I hadn't done it; but the handwriting is already on the wall.

Then there is the matter of blackjacking the lawyers into settlements, to clear the calendars and relieve congestion or to

171

get rid of some particularly complicated and troublesome case.

As a lawyer, whenever I had a case that did not look too good, I was hopeful that the judge might broach the subject of settlement. But when I had an exceptionally good case and went into court with a grim determination not to settle, it seemed as though fate was against me. We would get started and perhaps open to the jury and then the judge would call us up to the Bench and say, "Is there any possibility of a settlement?"

I would reply "No, your Honor, this is a case that cannot be settled."

Then a recess would be declared and the first thing I knew the judge had my client in his chambers. The discussion then proceeds in the corridor of the courthouse between me and my client:

Client: I think we had better settle.
Medina: No, we have a good case and we had better see it through.
Client: That is all very well for you to say. You are just the lawyer. But I have to pay if we lose; and the judge wants us to settle.

Result—the case was settled. I am exaggerating a little, but substantially that is about the way it would go.

As a lawyer I resented this. It seemed to me that the more complicated and difficult the case was, the more important it was for the judge to decide it; that it was one thing to accede to a request by the lawyers on both sides to facilitate settlement discussions but that the judge ought not to force the issue.

Now, the funny part of all this is I had not been a judge very long before I again did the very thing that I swore that I would never, never do. No, I would never blackjack anyone into a settlement, and I certainly would not call the clients into my

172

chambers without having the lawyers there too. Well, that is just what I did; and the settlement I am going to tell about is the one thing I am proudest about since I have been a judge.

The case was simple enough, but it was a son suing his mother. It had to do with some life-insurance policies. As I listened to the son testifying against his mother I made up my mind that this was simply something that I just could not permit to go on. If the case went to a conclusion, it was plain to me that the family ties would be forever broken and that there would remain scars which could never be eradicated.

And so I took a recess, first had a little powwow with the lawyers, and then began to work on the members of the family one by one: the son, the mother, the stepfather, and the little daughter-in-law. It was mighty tough going, but I took it easy and we came to the close of the first day without having made very much progress. Sometimes I would have them all in my chambers together and sometimes one at a time, with the lawyers in and the lawyers out. At one time during that first afternoon when I had all the members of the family there, I said something like this, "You know if we could really get this case settled, I think I could draw up some kind of a paper that all of you could sign which might help to keep things smooth for the future." Nobody seemed to be impressed by this, so the conversation went on and court adjourned for the day.

The next morning we went at it again and by lunchtime the ice was beginning to thaw. So I took them all out to lunch —on me—and, after feeding them a couple of cocktails apiece, it looked as though definite progress was possible. Without making too long a story of it, we had the case settled by about four o'clock and we went back into the courtroom and I dictated the terms of the settlement. As I turned to leave the Bench, these four people came up and the little daughter-in-law was the spokesman. She said: "Judge, do you remember that paper you said you might draw up?"

"Yes," I replied, "but I thought we decided to forget it."

"Well," she said, "we've been talking it over and we think we would like to have you do that and then if we felt like scrapping again, we could take out the paper and look at it and say, 'Judge Medina wouldn't like that,' and we would stop."

Well, I was really affected. It did seem as though, with a little patience and a little good will, something infinitely precious to the administration of justice was being accomplished.

And so here is how the paper read:

> With mutual forgiveness of all that is past and with a sincere resolve not to look back but ahead, in the spirit of the Golden Rule, we and each of us, now happily in affectionate accord, and earnestly desirous of remaining so, do solemnly promise that we will avoid all mention or discussion of matters large and small connected in any way with the proceedings which have just been terminated in a manner so satisfactory to all concerned.

They all signed and they got me to sign. There were five duplicate originals, no carbon copies, if you please. One of these originals went to the son, another to the mother, another to the stepfather, another to the daughter-in-law, and the last one to me. Each of these originals contained the signature of each of the five of us.

Here, again, I could go on indefinitely. Practically every resolution I formed before I became a judge has gone by the board. Things do look so different when, on the one hand, you are a lawyer practicing at the Bar and, on the other, when you are a judge sitting on the Bench trying your best to do justice.

Why, I even used to think the judges were lazy, whereas now, every time I see a judge ducking away from some piece of work I know in my heart that he is only trying to live another year or two and he has my sincere sympathy.

This is a good place to tie things together a bit. I am not telling you that it is foolish to make good resolutions because you are bound to break them. I am telling you about The Education of a Judge and how interesting it is to see the manipulation of man-made laws by human beings dealing with human material in the form of men and women coming into the courts for justice. Remember what I said about the humanities and about the human element in law. I am not sorry that I have not stuck to the letter of my good resolutions. I've kept them pretty well in spirit and I generally had good reasons for doing so when I broke them. But I'm not foolish enough to believe that I shall never make mistakes or that I shall not do things that I shall wish I hadn't done. All a man can do is his best, and if he makes a mistake, do his utmost to rectify it.

Now I come to the real meat of what I want to say. The most important thing I have learned as a judge is that the heart and soul of America are sound and true and that the intuitive judgment of the ordinary man in the street is in the aggregate something infinitely penetrating and reliable.

It is curious how wrong we can be, how again and again we fail to see the things that lie right before our eyes.

I have discovered by personal experience that there is in the heart of the common man, the average American one meets in the street and from one end of this great country of ours to the other, an intense and passionate interest in the administration of justice. I am an optimist and I have good reasons for being such; I believe in our country, I believe in its future, I believe in its people. The one thing we must fight with every fiber of our being is this infernal cynicism. When you once think everything is going to pot and that there is just nothing you can do about it you aren't worth a cuss.

When I became a judge the one thing I most feared was that I might become stuffy. It is so easy for a judge to become convinced of his own importance. Everyone keeps telling him what a wonderful person he is and the first thing you know he begins to believe it. From that moment he is a lost soul; and the worst of it is that even his friends will never tell him.

But so far I think I have done all right. Even before I was sworn in my wife was on the job. Every time we got in an argument she would say, "Don't be judgey. Don't be judgey."

I lost every argument. Now I have the answer. You know the judges' wives can put on a little dog themselves. Anyway, I get back at her by saying, "Don't be Mrs. Judgey," and I come out ahead once in a while.

Notes

THE pieces contained in this volume with the exception of "The Meaning of Freedom" were originally addresses delivered on the following occasions:

"A Look at America": The Economic Club of Detroit, April 18, 1955.

"The Influence of Woodrow Wilson on the Princeton Undergraduate, 1902–1910": Alumni Day, Princeton University, Princeton, New Jersey, February 18, 1956.

"The Meaning of Freedom": an impromptu expression composed in 1958 at the request of Dean Emeritus Clarence W. Mendell of Yale, published in *The Meaning of Freedom*, Freedom Fund, Inc., New York, copyright 1958.

"The Celebration of the Eightieth Birthday of Robert Frost": Waldorf-Astoria Hotel, New York City, March 25, 1954.

"The Liberal Arts and the Professions": Ferdinand Phinizy Lectures, University of Georgia, October 17 and 18, 1956.

"A Liberal Education and the Advancement of American Freedom": 1955 Convocation, Trinity College, Hartford, Connecticut.

"The Liberal Arts and the Whole Man": Seventy-Second anniversary of the opening of Rollins College, Winter Park, Florida, November 4, 1957.

"Patriotism": Eightieth Annual Washington's Birthday banquet of the Sons of the Revolution in the State of New York, Waldorf-Astoria, New York City, February 22, 1957.

"Argument Against Use of Television and Radio in Courtrooms": for CBS Television and Radio Broadcast, September 2, 1954.

"The Spiritual Quality of Justice": 1954 John Randolph Tucker Lectures, Washington and Lee University.

"Guts and Loyalty": commencement exercises of the FBI National Academy, Washington, D. C., November 16, 1956.

"Our Capacity for Growth": commencement exercises, University of Chattanooga, Chattanooga, Tennessee, September 2, 1952.

"Security": 153rd year commencement exercises, Middlebury College, Middlebury, Vermont, June 8, 1953.

"*In Litteris Libertas*": Bicentennial Anniversary of the Founding of the Columbia University Libraries, Butler Library, January 28, 1958.

"The Education of a Judge": annual meeting of the Virginia State Bar Association, White Sulphur Springs, West Virginia, August 9, 1952.